SONGS OF MY FAMILIES

SONGS

of My

FAMILIES

*A Thirty-Seven-Year Odyssey from
Korea to America and Back*

KELLY FERN
with Brad Fern

LANTERN BOOKS • NEW YORK
A Division of Booklight Inc.

2012
Lantern Books
128 Second Place
Brooklyn, NY 11231
www.lanternbooks.com

Printed in the United States of America

Print ISBN: 9781590563205
Ebook ISBN: 9781590563212

Library of Congress Cataloging-in-Publication Data

Fern, Kelly, 1967-
Songs of my families : a Thirty-Seven-Year odyssey from Korea to America and back / Kelly Fern with Brad Fern.
p. cm.
ISBN 978-1-59056-320-5 (alk. paper) — ISBN 978-1-59056-321-2 (ebook)
1. Fern, Kelly, 1967- 2. Fern, Kelly, 1967—Family. 3. Korean Americans—Biography. 4. Immigrants—United States—Biography. 5. Adopted children—Minnesota—Biography. 6. Orphans—Korea—Biography. 7. Teenage mothers—Minnesota—Biography. 8. Birthparents. 9. Family reunions. 10. Extended families. I. Fern, Brad. II. Title.
E185.K6F47 2012
305.895'7073—dc23
2011031878

MIX
Paper from
responsible sources
FSC® C011935

Lantern Books has elected to print this title on Rolland Enviro, a 100% post-consumer recycled paper, processed chlorine-free. As a result, we have saved the following resources:

7 trees, 837 lbs of solid waste, 6,618 gallons of water
11 million BTUs, and 2,175 lbs of greenhouse gases

As part of Lantern Books' commitment to the environment we have joined the Green Press Initiative, a non-profit organization supporting publishers in using fiber that is not sourced from ancient or endangered forests. We hope that you, the reader, will support Lantern and GPI in our endeavor to preserve the ancient forests and the natural systems on which all life depends. One way is to buy books that cost a little more but make a positive commitment to the environment not only in their words, but in the paper that they are published on. For more information, visit www.greenpressinitiative.org.

TO OUR SISTERS:

Pamela Fern and Kari Lee (Lee Hysugi)

Though your lives were short, the world is a far better place because you lived.

Acknowledgments

OVER TWENTY YEARS AGO I MET A LONG-HAIRED, BLUE-eyed, bohemian hairdresser named Brad. He and I started out as lovers and eventually became best friends. We traveled the world together, laughed and cried together, parented together, fought and broke up, made up and fell in love all over again. He encouraged me to embrace my past and to reclaim the fire. Thanks, Brad. I love you!

Thanks to Pam and Skip for welcoming me into their lives and for loving my precious baby. You are truly wonderful parents.

Thanks to Scott Edelstein whose skill, knowledge, and optimism made this book possible. Special thanks to Colleen Fern for providing moral support, and to the crew and staff at Korean Broadcasting System, who produced the wonderful documentary from my Korean family's point of view.

In order to protect some people, I have changed certain names and identifying features. Obviously, much of the dialogue from my childhood has been reconstructed from early recollections, and thus is not verbatim.

Finally, I'd like to thank my American parents for turning their lives upside-down to give me a home over four decades ago.

Contents

PART THREE: RETURN

⚬

Introduction

LUCKY

A S I WRITE THESE WORDS, I HAVE LIVED ON THIS EARTH
for forty-five years. For almost six of those years, I lived
in Korea with the name Myonghi. For the other forty years I've
lived in Minnesota with the name my American family gave me,
Kelly Jean. I believed that my biological mother was dead, that
I had no siblings, and that my Korean father had abandoned his
family to find a job in Seoul, never to return.

Five months before I began writing this book, because of
a one-page letter from Korean Social Service, I learned that I
had three older Korean sisters and two younger brothers. I discovered that my biological father was still alive and had never
abandoned the family. I found out that my mother gave me up
because we were all starving. I also learned that my family had
been searching for me for well over a decade.

It's hard to explain what it's like to be ripped from your family at five years old and sent to the opposite side of the planet,
to a place where nobody understands you and few people look
like you. I'm not sure I understand it myself.

When people find out that I was adopted from Korea, they

typically tell me how lucky I was to go from starving in Asia to thriving in America. And, generally, the sentiment is true. Times were hard in Korea. In our home, a few hours' car ride south of Seoul, all of my family slept in the same room on mats.

I vividly recall being four years old, crawling across the floor in the middle of the night to check my grandfather's mouth for food. My grandfather often made a chewing, smacking sound with his mouth when he was asleep. I knew before going over to him that his mouth was empty, but I was so hungry that I went anyway. I would whisper in Korean, "What are you chewing on, *Harabuzhĭ?*" Of course, he didn't answer, because he was sleeping. So, with that nagging, hollowness in my stomach, I'd quietly return back to my sleeping mat and dream of apples.

It's difficult to describe to someone who hasn't starved how you think about food all the time. Instead of wishing for toys or bicycles, you wish for rice or eggs. When food is available, you savor every morsel. Even today, I still have that feeling of poverty hanging over my head like a cloud, as if anything good is bound to end. There may be food to eat today and a warm place to stay tonight, but tomorrow, who knows?

I remember, when I was about four years old, walking down the gravel road by my house and seeing a rotten apple lying in the dirt. I must not have had anything to eat for quite a while because I had that bottomless feeling in my stomach. I picked up the apple and brushed it off, turning it until I found the least rotten part. Some of it was too nasty to eat, but I ate what I could and threw the rest away. I recall being sad that it was not a whole, fresh apple.

In other ways, however, I actually thrived in Korea. I remember the sound of river water running over stones and watching the sunlight dance across the rapids. My sisters and I washed the laundry in that beautiful river. My oldest sister's hands were supple, young, and strong as they worked the fabric against the rocks.

My sister would cook over a fire. Our kitchen was a small room separate from the rest of the house. You had to walk outside and around the corner to get to it. The kitchen was half exposed, I think. There was no door. On warmer days this allowed the heat out. The oven was made of clay, with a cast-iron top and a large opening in the front for the firewood. I would squat near the oven and stare into the fire as it grew. The flames would reach out of the opening, licking the air with their jagged tongues. Other times, we cooked over a fire in the yard. I loved helping, especially when we cooked my beloved eggs. I'd watch the flames tease the black pan as the eggs sizzled and turned white.

I'm thankful for those good memories of Korea, and I'm equally thankful for the American doctors who rebuilt my rotting teeth and deteriorating gums. I'm thankful for my American mother and father, who cared enough and had enough money to take care of my many physical problems, all brought on by malnutrition. I'm thankful for being treated for the intestinal parasites, and the modern medications I was given. And I'm thankful for my husband and my two children, whom I love beyond all imagining.

But when I hear that word "lucky," I sometimes want to ask, *What child feels lucky to give up their father, mother, sisters, and brothers?*

When I finally heard my Korean mother's voice again on the phone, when she cried so hard that she couldn't go on, and when my sister started to weep, too, so intensely she could barely speak, I knew how much I had been loved and how painful it was for them to let me go. I realized how much I had missed, and how my mother must have wept the day I was taken away.

Part One

EMIGRATION

One

THE LETTERS

A S AN ADULT, I'VE BEEN VERY QUIET ABOUT MY KOREAN past, even to my own family. However, my husband, Brad, is persistent, curious, and obstinate. For sixteen years, he pestered me about Korea. Most of the time I told him very little. Nonetheless, in 2002, he decided to bypass me and ask my American mother questions about my adoption. She told him that Lutheran Social Services had brought me over in coordination with Korean Social Service (KSS). She told him that I was supposed to be placed in a home in Minneapolis, and she said that the name of the family was Stephenson. That was it: three bits of information.

One night in 2003, Brad couldn't sleep. At around two in the morning, he sat at our computer and googled KSS. He took the phone number from the web site and called. It was daytime in Korea, and someone answered the phone immediately. Brad told the KSS representative my Korean name and asked her whether she could find any information about me or my family. The woman told him to call back in half an hour. When Brad called back, the woman had my file in her hand. I'd spent thirty-seven-years wondering about my Korean family, and my husband had found answers in under an hour. The phone conversation went as follows:

"Yes, Mr. Fern. Your wife was adopted in 1971, and she was sent to a home in Minneapolis, the Stephensons."

"No, I'm sorry," Brad interrupted. "That's *not* what happened. My wife was *supposed* to go to Minneapolis, but she ended up in Rochester. A flight attendant switched her sweater with one belonging to another little girl on the plane. Their identification information was pinned to those sweaters, so they both went to the wrong houses."

"Mr. Fern, we keep our files according to the names of the adopting families, and that's what our records show. I'm not allowed to give you any more information. If you don't mind, please write a letter and have your wife sign it. Then we will send you information about your wife's family."

That's what Brad did. He drafted a one-page synopsis of where I ended up and why. He wrote of how my new American mother fought to keep me, in addition to the other little girl and the baby that arrived weeks before I did. He explained that my little sister here in America had died when she was nineteen.

He mailed the letter to Korea in the summer of 2003. We didn't hear anything. Apparently, they filed the letter and nothing more was done about it.

Until four years later.

We received the letter on a sunny Saturday morning in August 2007. It had several cancellations from the Korean and American postal services and a number of words written in Korean characters in the return address. It was addressed to my husband.

It took me several moments before I could bring myself to open the envelope and unfold the letter. I read it out loud, with my husband listening.

AUGUST 25, 2007

Dear Mr. Brad Fern:

I am writing this letter in regard to your letter received in February of 2003 and feel sorry for having you kept waiting long. I appreciate your explanation why her last name was different than our record, and understand your interest in searching for your wife's Korean family. And I am very pleased to inform you that finally we have located the Korean family, which was happy to hear about your wishes.

The information on your wife's adoption background was very little so that it took time to locate and reach the Korean family. We have talked with the younger brother, Chulsoo, on the phone. According to him the birth parents were married, having five children and your wife was born the fourth child. But at the time her father's health condition was not good and the economic situation was bad so the parents asked to the orphanage for your wife's adoption.

In Korea she has three older sisters and two younger brothers, one brother being born after she left. All family members including both parents are doing well and want to know how your family is doing. I really hope your mailing address is still available and look forward to hearing from you soon for your wife's Korean family. Thank you for your patience and understanding.

Best regards!

Sincerely,

Ms. Kim

It wasn't real. They must have made a mistake. Tens of thousands of Koreans made the trip across the Pacific just like me. They must have mixed me up with someone else, or maybe Brad had given them the wrong information.

"Oh my God!" Brad exclaimed. "There's been a family back there waiting for you all this time."

Brad was obviously excited. He went on and on about the possibilities. I tuned him out and went numb. Within hours, I had put the idea of a Korean family on a shelf and went on with my business, as if the letter had never been delivered.

A few days later, however, I brought in the mail and tossed it onto the dining room table. Ms. Kim's follow-up letter fell separately, seemingly jumping out from the rest. This one was addressed to me.

WEDNESDAY, AUGUST 29, 2007

Dear Mrs. Kelly Jean,

I have talked with your brother about this contact from you and got the permission to give you the contact information on your brother, Chulsoo, who is living with your parents.

Chulsoo (younger brother): (0) 09-72-22-85

According to him, he has poor English so you may need a translator to contact him. Hope you to keep in touch with them. Best regards!

Sincerely,

Ms. Kim

My heart felt like it was going to fly out of my chest. The tips of my fingers tingled. It began to dawn on me that what had happened might be real. I had a name and a phone number. At any time, I could pick up the phone and call my Korean brother. I tried to imagine what he might look like, what it would be like for him to walk down a street in Seoul and have his long-lost sister call. I imagined a large, bottomless well. I pictured my whole history falling away into the darkness. I felt a small hunger pang in my stomach, and went into the kitchen for something to eat.

Two

THE ORPHANAGE

O NE DAY WHEN I WAS ABOUT FIVE YEARS OLD, A WOMAN came in a car to take me away. She must have been an American from Lutheran Social Services, because she was wearing a skirt, and in the early 1970s most Korean women didn't show their legs. At least they didn't in the rural area I was from. She must have been wearing nylons because I couldn't stop staring at the sheen of her skin. Her shins looked like they were made of plastic.

The car was huge. I had seen cars drive by, but it was my first time inside one. When the door closed and it was only the woman and me inside, I started to panic. I tried to get out of the car, but I was too small. I cried and called out for my mother, and then watched my Korean life vanish behind me in the back window.

The orphanage was large, scary, and official looking. We called the women who took care of us "sisters." They were often rough and didn't show much compassion. They weren't cruel, but they weren't nurturing, either. After I saw other girls punished, I quickly realized that acting different was a bad idea. I'm still angry at the orphanage workers when I think of how they treated me, but I understand now that they were probably over-whelmed by the number of children they were responsible for.

Two of my friends in America are Korean adoptees. They talk about how their heads were shaved because of lice and how poorly they were treated because they no longer had families. Koreans judge themselves by how well they fill predetermined roles in their society and family. When you have no genetic parents, you can't be a daughter or a son. You're nobody's child. That's why so many Korean orphans were sent to America. In America, it's all about individuality. Americans judge themselves by how they carve out unique roles for themselves, regardless of blood ties or circumstances.

No one ever shaved my head at the orphanage where I stayed, but I was rarely fed much more than rice and broth. From time to time, we were given crackers. This was a step down from the food my Korean family had fed me. I was so underfed that eventually my stomach became bloated.

The sisters would also feed us powdery yellow tablets, which were probably vitamins. I can still see the big white plastic bottle they came in. I hated the smell, which was like musty, uncooked macaroni, but at least the tablets were something to eat. To this day, I can taste the bitterness they left on my tongue.

I remember a large room with yellow floors. One sister would walk around dispensing those horrible pills. A second sister always followed the first, letting each child drink water from a ladle dipped into a bucket. When it was time for a shower, we'd stand in a line, naked. My teeth chattered from the cold, and the dirt on my skin built up in water droplets like oblong beads. When the sisters were finished, we'd been scrubbed so hard that we looked like muddy lobsters. Then a cold blast of water would rinse away the soap and grime.

On the coldest days, the sisters gave us baths. One at a time, we'd step into the water and the sisters would scrub us with rough, red mitts that felt like sandpaper. The bathwater had to be changed when one of the children had an accident, and the rest of us had to watch as the sisters spanked the guilty child's bottom or smacked her hands with a ruler. I hated those bathing sessions, but sometimes when I stood just outside of the washing area I could look down the hill at Seoul below. I would peek at the city when it was lit up at night and fantasize about the well-fed, happy families living in those beautiful, lighted buildings.

Even at that young age I understood that the orphanage was just a stopping point along my journey. I knew somehow that I wasn't going home and something very different, but worthwhile, awaited me in the future.

My best friend at the orphanage was Hyogi. She was a year younger than me, and always talked about her baby sister and how the two of them were going to live together in America. She and I would play doctor, or use pebbles and sticks to construct houses or draw faces, outside the main building. I cringe at the thought now, but I would mix spit with dirt and call it medicine, and spit into her mouth and challenge Hyogi to swallow her medicine.

Hyogi's mother visited the orphanage several times, bringing candy, fruit, and other treats for her to eat. At these times, I'd miss my Korean family. I'd wonder why they didn't visit me and bring me treats like Hyogi's mother did.

In an orphanage you're not alone when you cry at night. You can hear the sniffles and subdued weeping around you. I'd often lie in bed, thinking about what would become of me. I especially missed my father. I prayed to Buddha that my father would appear one day and offer gifts and say he was sorry for letting me go. He'd explain that it was all a big misunderstanding and beg me to come back, and plead with me to be his daughter again. And I would jump up and hug him and kiss him. Then he would take me home.

I wanted so much for him to come, take my hand, and guide me through this cold, confusing world.

Three

LEAVING KOREA

S OUTH AND NORTH KOREA BECAME COUNTRIES IN 1945, about twenty years before I was born. The original plan was for the Soviet Union to administer the northern half of the Korean peninsula and the United States the south, until the two superpowers agreed on terms of reunification. That agreement was never fulfilled. Separate governments formed, both claiming to be the legitimate authority for the whole of Korea.

In the summer of 1950, with the blessing of Joseph Stalin, the North invaded the South in an attempt to bring all of Korea under communist rule. The town where I lived was directly in the invasion's path. The United States and the Soviet Union escalated the conflict by pouring in advisors, money, and soldiers. China sent in thousands of troops to fight on behalf of the North and called it "the War to Resist America and Aid Korea." North Korea called it "the Fatherland Liberation War." The United States, working under the auspices of the United Nations, called it a police action. I call it a tragedy.

The United States dropped hundreds of thousands of tons of bombs and some thirty tons of napalm on Korea. Three million Koreans were killed. Over 30,000 Americans lost their lives and 130,000 Chinese died. When the North Korean army was finally stopped by the American and South Korean forces, it retreated, massacring tens of thousands of prisoners of war and civilians as it withdrew. Many bodies were dumped in mass graves, some with their hands tied behind their backs and bullet holes in their skulls. My hometown was in the path of this bloody retreat.

An armistice was signed in the summer of 1953, thirteen years before I was born. The two new countries established a tense equilibrium, but the war had crippled both economies, devastated communities, and left much of the Korean peninsula in ruins. Thousands of families were torn apart. The Korean people, including my family, spent the late fifties and early sixties recovering from that civil war.

Today, South Korea has a booming economy and is a modern country. However, in the winter of 1971 it was one of Asia's poorest nations—so poor that many families, including mine, couldn't feed their own children, and were forced to give them up.

On December 18, 1971, Hyogi and I were put on a plane of Korean adoptees headed for America. I was five years old. I don't remember much about the flight, except that it was hot and stuffy and that I slept most of the way. We flew over the Pacific Ocean and stopped for an hour or two in Hawaii. A very sweet flight attendant gave me and Hyogi a big smile, and helped us take off our sweaters. Then I wasn't so hot or uncomfortable. When the plane took off again, Hyogi and I leaned on each other, and we spent the flight falling in and out of sleep.

When the plane began its descent into Minneapolis, another flight attendant attempted to put Hyogi's sweater on me. I tried to explain, "That's not my sweater," but the woman didn't speak Korean. I had been taught never to disrespect elders, so I let her stretch the sweater over my head. The collar was tight and the sleeves didn't reach down to my wrists, but she didn't notice. Then she put my sweater on Hyogi.

The only things identifying both of us were the nametags on those sweaters. That young woman had just changed my name, my community, my family, and my future.

We landed in Minneapolis on December 19 at three o'clock in the morning. The temperature was in the low teens, Fahrenheit. The orphanage had provided me with bright red shoes, one of which was several sizes too big. The loose shoe forced me to drag my right foot, and when I reached some stairs I had to curl my toes and slide my foot down. It must have looked like I had a terrible limp.

I barely remember my new American mother that day, but I have a picture of her and my new family. She is smiling, thrilled to meet her new daughter. My new brother looks tired, but is smiling, too. My new baby sister is asleep. I'm looking away from the others with a dazed, forlorn expression. I'm wearing plaid, knee-high pants, red socks, and that gray sweater. My new mother's hand is draped over my shoulder, with her two fingers hanging over the nametag that identifies me as Hyogi. My American father isn't in the picture. He must have been on the other side of the camera.

I tried to stay awake during the car ride from Minneapolis to Rochester, but my head and limbs felt heavy and my eyes flitted like a camera shutter. Finally, I gave in and fell asleep.

The house in Rochester dazzled me. It seemed to go on forever. There were so many lights and beautiful furniture everywhere. The house had yellow carpeting, a big white couch, and two king-and-queen-style green velvet chairs.

The walls of my bedroom had pink, green, and yellow striped wallpaper. The lamp was covered in white cotton fabric. I'd never slept on anything but a mat before, so the bed seemed so high that it scared me. The design on the wicker headboard reminded me of a peacock's tail, and the mattress was covered by a luxurious white spread. The bed had a large bump near one end that I would later learn was a soft, feather-filled pillow. I'd never seen a pillow before. Everything was illuminated by the soft glow from a hanging lamp in the corner. It was the most magnificent room I'd ever seen.

My new mother couldn't have been more kind. She held me as much as I would let her, and she stayed with me until I felt safe. Then she sat on the bed and pulled the covers back, but I wouldn't get in. I didn't want to risk trying to balance through the night without falling off that huge bed. The mattress was far too soft, and there was all that fabric for me to get lost in. I felt the cottony, pink rug on the floor beneath my feet and looked down. It reminded me of the mats I'd slept on all of my five-and-a-half years. That first night in my new American bedroom, I slept on the floor with the light from the lamp bathing the room to comfort me. My new mother sat at my side until I closed my eyes.

I woke up in the middle of the night, not knowing where I was. I looked around at all of the abundance. The silence was so harsh and I felt so alone. I finally realized I wasn't going home again, and I cried. I missed my Korean family, but, by that time, my memories of them were already starting to fade. It had been a long time since we'd lived together. The room I was sleeping in was the size of our entire living space in Korea. So much about my Korean life just didn't feel real anymore.

The next morning my new mother came into my bedroom to check on me. I wasn't on the rug or in the bed, and she started to panic. Finally, she decided to look under the bed. There I was, fast asleep, in a place that felt secure and safe.

Four

MY NEW HOME IN AMERICA

THOSE FIRST FEW DAYS IN AMERICA BROUGHT ONE MIR-
acle after another. The biggest and best was the refrigerator,
a magical box as big as a closet. A light went on each time I
opened the door, and I'd open and close it over and over again,
trying to see how the light knew when to go on and turn off. It
was mysteriously cold inside and held more food than a whole
Korean family could eat in a month. Many of the foods I'd never
seen before.

Apples, however, were a food that I knew well. My American
mother remembers watching me walk around the house with
an apple, and wondering how I took hours to eat only one. She
didn't realize it wasn't one apple. I ate the whole bag, one by
one, and ended up with a horrible stomachache. One morning,
my mother went to get eggs from the fridge and discovered that
I'd poked holes in the shells, sucked out all the insides, and then
put the empty shells back in the carton. That was the reason for
another stomachache and the diarrhea that went with it.

I remember not wanting sweets like the other kids when I
first arrived. I wanted meat, fruits, and vegetables. I remember

throwing myself on the floor and screaming, *"Koegee, koegee!"* What I wanted was Korean barbeque beef, a traditional dish. My mother offered me a cookie, but I refused. Eventually my mother called a young Korean girl who lived a few blocks from us. She'd been adopted at the age of eleven, so she still spoke Korean. She knew right away that I just wanted a piece of meat. My mother dug through the fridge, searching for something to give me. She pulled out a hotdog and offered it to me. It wasn't what I expected. It wasn't the thin sliced beef or pork that I'd eaten in Korea, but it was meat after all.

There was another magical box in another room: the television. It had a window in the front and people would talk to you through it. I kept jumping behind, trying to see the people from the other side, but I could only see them through the little window. They only wanted to talk and didn't listen to anything I said. I waved, jumped up and down, and even shouted at them, but they just went about their business.

Eventually, I grew to love a local children's television show called *Captain Kangaroo*. The captain was a sweet, grandfatherly Caucasian man who showed kids how to draw, make paper animals, and other fun activities. I used to get out of bed early just to watch his show. I loved his friendly face and big mustache. His gentle voice was always so calming.

Another amazement was the bathroom. I couldn't believe that I didn't have to leave the house to take a bath or relieve myself. It was warm and clean and didn't stink, and you could flush your business out of sight when you were finished.

Within days, my mother took me to a shopping mall. I couldn't get over all the toys. There were things there I never dreamed existed. There was so much to see, so much to have, so much to want.

It wasn't long before I was showered with Christmas gifts. So was Hysugi, my new baby sister. Aunts, uncles, grandparents—everybody gave us presents. I unwrapped one pretty box after another, but I didn't understand at first that I could keep what was inside. I received more gifts in this one holiday than I had in all of my five-and-a-half years.

When I had seen my new baby sister at the airport that first day in Minneapolis, I knew immediately that a mistake had been made. My friend Hyogi had told me that she would be reunited with her little sister Hysugi in America, but when she got off the plane, she was shown to a smiling American couple and led away. And here was Hysugi with my own new family. Yet none of the adults around me seemed to notice, and I was too tired, confused, and frightened to say anything. I felt sad knowing that Hyogi was waiting somewhere to be reunited with her baby sister, but was glad that Hysugi would be part of my family instead.

Within my first week in America, I felt comfortable enough to try to explain the problem. "This is Hysugi," I said in Korean, "and she is not my sister. She is the baby sister of my friend Hyogi. We were good friends at the orphanage. This is not my sister."

I pointed at Hysugi, speaking slowly and enunciating each of my words. With my hand extended in front of me and pointing at Hysugi, I shook my head repeatedly. My mother looked at me with a confused smile. The message was not getting through. I moved closer to the baby and moved my extended index finger back and forth between Hysugi in the crib and my chest.

"This baby is not my sister." I shook my head more emphatically. "This . . . is . . . not . . . my . . . sister."

But there was no reaction, just a gentle hand on my head, sliding down past my ear and onto my shoulder as a caress.

Hysugi was about eighteen months old. I leaned over and spoke into her beautiful, doll-like face. "Your big sister is waiting to see you, Hysugi. She always talked a lot about you at the orphanage and about how excited she was to come live with you in America. Your sister and I played games together. She must be very sad that you are not with her."

Hysugi didn't respond, and I knew that she had already gotten used to English and didn't understand Korean anymore.

It wasn't long before my mother started to suspect that something had gone wrong. Korean Social Service had sent pictures of Hyogi and little Hysugi ahead of time. My mother held Hyogi's picture up, comparing me to her image. I was a year older and taller. My ears were different, and there were distinct differences in our facial features. My hair was thicker and coarser.

I'd been in America about a month when my new parents finally realized that they'd been given the wrong child and that their two new children were not biologically related. But in the very short time we'd been together, a loving bond had already formed, and I was starting to feel at home in my new world.

Not long after my arrival, I needed to have surgery on my mouth. My molars were rotten and hollow, and my mouth bled all the time, causing me great pain whenever I chewed. So, my mother packed an overnight bag and took me to St. Mary's Hospital, where my horrible teeth could be fixed.

A nurse checked us in and we were led to a room with a bed. Something seemed strange about that room, but my new mother was with me, so I obediently took off my clothes and donned the small hospital robe, like the nurse told me to.

There were many strange things in this bedroom. I had just gotten used to the bed at home, but the bed in this room was even higher off the floor. It had a shiny metal arm over it. You could press buttons to make the mattress go up and down. Someone had fastened a television on the wall, and there was a second bed behind a curtain, with several chairs around it. The room also had its own bathroom. But I wasn't impressed. It wasn't a pretty room, and it smelled awful.

The nurse and doctor were very kind. They smiled and their voices were soft and considerate. They wanted to touch me, and I started to enjoy the attention.

Then the doctor turned around. He was obviously trying to hide something from me. My mother and the nurse went from talking spontaneously to trying to distract me. When the doctor turned back, I got a glimpse of the needle he was holding in his hand.

I was terrified. I'd been given shots in Korea. They'd all been very painful, and one had become infected and had left a quarter-sized scar on my arm. I tried to run.

My mother grabbed me, and tried to calm me by rubbing my hand. Another nurse entered the room, and the two nurses took hold of my legs. I screamed until two other nurses ran in and held my arms. I wriggled and strained and kicked, and just as I thought I was about to break free, a fifth nurse entered. They pinned me to the bed. The needle went in, and I went to sleep.

The next morning my mother greeted me with a smile. She'd sat beside my bed the entire night. In addition to keeping watch over me, she'd knitted a little purse. It had a delicate flower design and was lined with cotton. I knew immediately that she'd worked the whole night to make it for me. I loved that purse. I still have it today, and now my daughter plays with it.

A nurse entered the room with a mirror. She asked me to open my mouth and held the mirror in front of my face. The surgeons had capped my black, rotting, hollow teeth with silver.

I said the only English word that I could think of: "Pretty."

The Stephensons had grown attached to Hyogi and didn't want to give her up. Hyogi had been with them for six months, and, understandably, they had they bonded with her, just as my new parents had with me. There was some suggestion that I would go to the Stephensons and Hyogi would go to my family. But my mother decided that she wasn't going to swap daughters. She wanted Hyogi, Hysugi, *and* me.

There was also talk about driving to Minneapolis to argue in court. My mother's phone conversations with the adoption agency were polite, but I could see the strain in her face and hear it in her voice. She is a very reserved and polite person, but she became more anxious with every day that Hysugi was separated from her biological sister. I could tell she was uneasy just by the stiffness of her walk and the way she'd slam doors and speak briskly to my American father.

The court date was set and my parents and the Stephensons prepared for a custody battle. But it never happened. The Stephensons realized that the two biological sisters ought to be together, and they agreed to let Hyogi join my family. They also let me remain with my new family.

The whole affair must have been very painful for my mother. She was acting in the best interest of the three adopted children, but she must have also imagined how difficult it was for the Stephensons. I'm sure she suffered some sleepless nights worrying about how they felt. Throughout the whole process, I never felt like I was in danger of being given up again. My new parents made it clear that I was a family member, and I was going to stay with them.

I had learned English surprisingly well by then.

"You know, Kelly," my mother said, "it's going to be very hard on Hyogi to separate from the Stephensons. We have to be gentle with her and make her feel at home. She might be sad and cry a lot."

"Why is it hard on her?" I asked.

"Because this will be the second time that she's been taken from a family. We are going to be her third family. That's very hard for anyone, especially a five-year-old."

It was a sunny spring day when we went to pick Hyogi up in our station wagon. I remember leaning against the car, waiting for everyone, so we could leave. My mother had made me wear a dress.

Little Hysugi wore a white dress. My brother was dressed in slacks and a shirt. He liked to joke a lot, always composing funny rhymes and word games. He also enjoyed giving us piggyback rides. But he wasn't saying much that day. He was waiting like the rest of us to see what would happen.

When we arrived at the courthouse, my parents told my brother and sister and me to stay in the car. While they were inside, we watched some of the previous fall's leaves blow around. The inside of the car got so hot that we slipped out and sat on the grass.

I recognized Hyogi right away. Her hair had grown to shoulder length, and it was a darker black than I remembered. She looked upset, but it was good to see her anyway. I stepped aside, knowing that she would want to see her baby sister most.

She flung her arms around little Hysugi and kissed her. "Hysugi! Hysugi! Hysugi! My baby sister! She is mine!"

Hysugi was not as excited about the reunion as Hyogi. She tried to pull away and protested with an angry whine.

"Hysugi! This is my baby sister! She is mine!"

Hyogi sat in the car next to Hysugi, holding her hand. Hysugi tried to pull her hand free from time to time, but Hyogi wouldn't let go.

I was happy for them both. After a while, Hyogi turned to me and smiled. I smiled back. I was happy to see her face. I asked her what kind of food she ate at the Stephensons'. We talked for a while and, before I knew it, we were home again.

That first night, Hyogi and I lay in bed, speaking a mix of English and Korean. The Stephensons had given her a yellow doll with a large head and black, round dots for eyes. The head of the doll was almost as big as Hyogi's.

"I like your doll," I said.

"I like him, too. His name is Mr. Smiley because he has a big smile."

"Did you have a television?" I asked.

"Yes, we had one."

"We have one, too. And we have a dishwasher."

"We had a dishwasher," Hyogi said. "Do you have a vacuum cleaner?"

"Yep."

"Does your mother cook?"

"Yes, she's good at cooking."

"My mother let us eat candy and have as much gum as we wanted," said Hyogi. "Do you get candy?"

"No. Well, sometimes."

"I learned an American song."

"What is it?"

"I'll show you." And Hyogi began to sing:

My bonnie lies over the ocean.
My bonnie lies over the sea.
My bonnie lies over the ocean.

Oh bring back my bonnie to me.
Bring back, bring back,
Oh bring back my bonnie to me, to me.
Bring back, bring back,
Oh bring back my bonnie to me.

"What a great song," I said. "Can you teach it to me?"
She did, and we sang it together.
"What were the Stephensons like?" I asked.
"They were nice. My father smoked, so the whole house smelled like ashes. I always wondered what happened to Hysugi, though. I missed her so much."
We fell asleep that night talking about our shared past in Korea and our new lives in America.
Hyogi followed Hysugi around for the first few days, always holding her hand or caressing her cheeks. Eventually, she started to relax and get into her own routine.
We often played in the park just behind our yard or in the neighborhood yards. We'd play games like softball, kick the can, and ollie ollie in come free on the streets with our new American friends. In the summer, we'd stay outside all day and go home only to eat. My mother would ring a cowbell when it was time for lunch, and we'd come running. Then we'd play outside again until it got dark. We were American children now, living the quintessential American life.

Four years after Hyogi became my sister, on Friday, September 17, 1976, we became U.S. citizens. It was unusual for three adopted sisters to be sworn in at once, so we made the front page of the local paper. The headline read, "3 CITY GIRLS JOIN 150

STATE RESIDENTS AS NEW CITIZENS." The picture was of the three of us holding little American flags.

We went off to the courthouse in Minneapolis for the swearing-in ceremony. I remember the judge in his long black gown. He had silver hair and a deep voice. He took us up with him on the lectern and let us stand with him while my parents took pictures of their three American daughters. My parents were so proud.

Five

AN AMERICAN LIFE

I N MANY WAYS I HAD A CLASSIC, SMALL-TOWN AMERICAN upbringing. We lived in a residential neighborhood of Rochester, Minnesota, with lots of trees and perfect lawns. The children addressed the adults by their first names, which would be unthinkable in Korea. Everyone had cars and there were lots of nice houses, even some with picket fences.

My father has a degree in education. He is retired now, but he was an elementary school teacher for most of his life. He served in the air force in the 1950s, but never flew planes or fought in a war. Born in a small, Iowa farm town, he was the third of four children. His father owned a farm implement business. My father is a pious man, dedicated to his church and his community. He loves to bake bread and pies, and he is especially gifted at growing beautiful flowers.

My mother was an early-education teacher. She earned a bachelor's degree with a teaching certificate, and she worked with preschool children. When she was young, she and her family lived in Germany and Japan. Her father was an administrator of American military schools after World War II. My mother is extremely good at seeing the value in old things—furniture and pictures, and so on. She can take a broken-down old chair and turn it into a treasure. She collects dolls and loves to travel.

On a perfect August day in 1972, my father held my hand and walked me to my first day of kindergarten, at Elton Hills Elementary. The sun was shining, and there wasn't a cloud in the sky. I was so proud of my new sundress. It was pink and yellow with white lace trim. I was too new to America to understand what school was; I just knew that there would be other children there, and I could hardly wait to play.

My new teacher was very beautiful. When I walked into the classroom, she bent down on one knee so she could look me in the eye. She greeted me with a big smile, and I knew that I was going to feel at home there. She gave us snacks every day, and we took naps on mats, just like in Korea. I was so excited.

The school administration provided me with a speech therapist. It had been seven months since I'd begun to speak English, and I was communicating pretty well. But I still couldn't manage my *L*'s and *R*'s. I felt very special when the therapist worked with me.

I was a social butterfly in school and got in trouble for talking too much. I made lots of friends and loved to paint and draw.

Unfortunately, my race was an issue for some of the other children. In the fourth grade, I went to school with two mean boys named Tom and Darren. Darren would often taunt me by whispering racial slurs. "I don't like chinks," he would say as I walked by.

One day, I could see that Darren and Tom were getting into some kind of trouble.

"You'd better not say anything, you Jap!" Tom said angrily. Then he took his scissors and slashed my hand with the blade. "You'd better not say anything, or I'll get you even worse."

The cut was deep. I realized that he wasn't joking around, that he really would hurt me seriously if I told on him. I got a bandage to stop the bleeding, and I cried. But I never told the teacher. I have the scar on my hand to this day.

That same year, I came home from school one day to find two boys and a girl waiting for me in my front yard. One of the boys was my age and about my height. The other was a year older and about six inches taller than me. I could tell by their faces and their aggressive postures that they'd come to harass me.

"Hey you!" the older boy called out, as I walked up and stood face-to-face with him.

"Are you talking to me?" I said.

"Yeah, you, chink. Who'd ya think I was talking to?"

I've always been astonished how stupid bigots can be. "Chink" is a derogatory word for a Chinese person, and "Jap" is a derogatory word for a Japanese person. In America, if you want to insult a Korean, the word is "Gook." But I didn't tell him that.

"Get off my lawn!" I demanded, as the anger surged through my body.

"Who's gonna make me?"

The other two laughed out loud, as if it was the best joke they'd ever heard. I suddenly realized that he was, in fact, too big for me to physically push off the grass.

"I'm going in to tell my parents if you don't get off now," I said.

The small boy stepped forward, grabbed my arm, and bit it. I felt the pain as his teeth clamped down, and I panicked. I jerked my arm away, took his arm, and bit him right back. Then I stomped on his foot as hard as I could, and pushed him down. He got up crying, and ran home. The other two became scared and hightailed it, too. I ran into the house and straight to my room. The place where the boy had bit me hurt so much.

Looking back, it's strange that all I worried about was how I was going to explain to my parents what I'd done. I felt guilty.

Because my father was a teacher, he had three months' vacation each year. Our family was able to travel for weeks at a time, and each year we toured a different part of the United States in a pickup truck camper. It had a small kitchenette with a refrigerator and several cleverly tucked-away beds. My sisters and I slept on the top bed, my parents slept on the fold-down kitchen bed, and my brother slept on the floor. When we were on the road, my mother would often have food cooking in the oven so we could pull over and eat dinner, without incurring the expense of going out to eat.

I saw the Rocky Mountains and visited Balancing Rock in North Dakota. We went to the Badlands, Disneyland, Yosemite National Park in California, and—on one of our last trips as a family together—to Knoxville, Tennessee, for the 1982 World's Fair.

Pictures don't do the Rocky Mountains justice. Their snowy peaks dominate the horizon for miles as you approach on the highways from the east, and when you're near to them you practically have to bend your spine backward to take them all in from the ground to the sky. We hiked the trails and often found ourselves hugging the mountain walls to let others pass, lest we make one wrong move and fall hundreds of feet. The mountains around my Korean home were gentler and didn't have the sheer cliffs or the snow at their summits.

I remember feeling the mist of the Yosemite's Old Faithful geyser against my face. I wrinkled my nose at its sulfur smell. Another summer, I stood in awe at the foot of one of the glaciers in Glacier National Park, thinking of the hundreds of millions of tons of packed snow and ice.

When I was ten, we visited my mother's parents in Hawaii

for five weeks. On the way over, the airline bumped us up to first class. I was in heaven. The huge leather seats, shrimp cocktails, and the pretty flight attendants made me feel like a princess. My mother's father was my favorite grandparent. He always made me feel important. My grandmother suffered from arthritis. I remember her using a walker and later a wheelchair. There were lush greens and beautiful flowers everywhere around their home—as well as lots of dark-skinned native people and Asians. It was nice to see so many people who looked like me.

My grandpa welcomed us with fresh leis around our necks. He took us to see Pearl Harbor, volcanoes and reefs, and so much more. We went to a restaurant that hung from the side of a cliff over the ocean. I had never eaten in such a fancy place. I wanted to stay in Hawaii forever. I had landed in Hawaii on my way to America only five years earlier and probably had even landed at the same airport. That fact was always in the back of my mind. My old Korean home and my Korean family were only hours away. By then, however, my first five years were a dream that I didn't trust anymore.

Some of our Minnesota summer camping trips were organized with other families who had adopted Korean children. At times, there were six families or more at a gathering. We swam, picked berries, and hiked. We got our feet dirty in the mud and roasted marshmallows. It was nice to socialize with other Korean kids. It was comforting to know my sisters and I weren't the only ones.

I can remember other parents talking about how Koreans did not give up boys. I figured that this couldn't be true. *Why would Korean families want to give up the girls?* I thought. *Everybody knew that girls were smarter than boys.* Besides, I noted, there were several boys in the Korean adoptees group. I remember one boy in particular because he had a glass eye.

In the evening, we sat around the fire roasting marshmallows and talking until it was late. I loved getting up early and checking to see if the embers of last night's fires were still hot. I would gather kindling and restart the fire until it was blazing again. I was so proud that everyone could enjoy the warmth because of what I'd done.

Hyogi, Hysugi, and I were close. The summer road trips taught us about our new country while giving us time together to become sisters. My love for the two of them grew very strong. My Caucasian brother was my parents' only biological child, and he was quite a bit older than us. He came along on the earlier trips, but by the time he was sixteen he often stayed at home by himself. That was when he grew his hair long and started playing the guitar, joining bands, and hanging out with his musician friends. I thought he was so cool.

As it is with every life, some events and circumstances in my American life were difficult. There's an old saying, "That which does not kill you will make you stronger." Not long after my first day of school, a neighbor boy started molesting me—and did so repeatedly for six years. Months would go by without him visiting, and I'd think it was over. Then he'd come back into our house and the nightmare would resume.

He was six years older than I was. If I told on him, he threatened, my American parents would send me back to Korea, and then I'd have no family at all. At one point, I tried telling my parents, but they didn't get the message. Children are often inarticulate, especially about abuse. By the time I considered myself a full member of the family, my spirit had been beaten down, and I was unable to stand up for myself. So the abuse continued and became part of my life. I felt I had to endure it even though it was tearing me apart inside.

Sometimes, he would sleep over at our house. He'd enter my room in the middle of the night, and I'd lie there, pretending to sleep, holding my breath and clenching all of the muscles in my body. The touch of his hands made me want to die. They afflicted every part of me. I'd fall unconscious, or would go deep inside myself to some imaginary place far away. When he'd finish I'd come back, and sometimes cry myself to sleep.

Sometimes he'd catch me in the bathroom. He'd force me to lie on the floor with my pants down and my stomach facing upward and bare, and he'd climb on top of me. It was on that bathroom floor that he introduced me to a shame so profound that I wouldn't be able to let it go for decades. I remember looking up at the bathroom ceiling; the neatly folded towels hanging down from the rack; the underside of the vanity top; the spider in the corner clinging to its web between the wall and ceiling, holding perfectly still.

During those years I prayed very hard that I wouldn't be sent to hell. God was so angry at me. I was doing something horrible.

The first few times, I was disgusted that he'd spat on me. I couldn't figure out how the spit ended up on my stomach without coming from his mouth. I didn't understand. I knew we were doing something dirty, but I wasn't about to give up my new family. I had to allow it.

"They won't believe you," he said. "They'll blame you and send you back. And then you'll have nobody."

Something inside me thought he was right. They wouldn't believe me. Why would they? He'd lived his whole life in America. I was a guest in his world.

The pain of the sexual abuse was too much to bear. I'd sometimes weep for hours. It felt like I had no control over my body.

It wasn't until my twelfth year that I finally gathered the strength to stop him. He was almost eighteen by then. I couldn't take it anymore. The guilt and disgust were rotting my soul. The way that it ended was really quite simple.

"Please, please stop," I said. "I can't take it anymore. Please stop."

I begged, almost like I was dying and my last breath was coming out. He didn't say anything. He simply got up and walked out. It was finally over.

But he'd already broken me.

When I'd arrived in the United States, I was a spirited, energetic, and outgoing child. After years of sexual abuse, I was an emotional wreck. I felt guilty for what had happened, as if it was my fault. I became depressed and unable to concentrate on schoolwork or to make simple, logical choices. I was convinced that God hated me.

During my fourteenth year, my brother hid a bottle of whisky in his closet. I found it and drank the whole thing—not to get drunk, but in the hope that it would kill me. Another time, I took two belts, and tied one around a pipe in the basement, and another round my neck. I set a chair underneath the pipe, and was on the verge of hanging myself before I pulled away at the last minute. I couldn't go through with it.

My life at school started to deteriorate. Junior high was painful. Like all children can be at times, the girls were cruel. It wasn't a good time to be different. I can remember the hot feeling in my cheeks when someone would yell out, "Hey, chink!" I knew they were talking to me. I'd usually turn as if I didn't notice the racial slur.

Once I was in the locker room with about six girls who were singing the popular song "Turning Japanese" by The Vapors. While one girl sang, she took her index fingers and slanted her eyes till they were almost closed. As she did so, she turned toward me and laughed. I felt like someone had hit me in the stomach with a rock. Why couldn't they let me forget that I was different?

My downward spiral started the day I decided to smoke a cigarette in the girls' bathroom. I was caught and suspended. By that time, I was smoking pot, partying, and lying to my parents about boys. I trusted no one.

My high school career lasted only a few days before I walked out and never went back. Not long after that, my parents said they were taking me to a dentist appointment, and we got into the family car. After we'd traveled well beyond the dentist's office, my parents told me they were putting me into a treatment facility. We drove through the farm fields of southern Minnesota to a hospital in Minneapolis. I didn't resist. I thought I should at least give treatment a chance. My life wasn't exactly perfect.

I lasted a couple of weeks in the hospital program. Then I was transferred to a long-term facility, where I lived for six months. At first, I felt isolated, until I started getting to know the other residents. I became close to one girl about my age, Dawn, and we remained friends long after our treatment experiences were over. She was shy and came from a poor family, and was truly chemically dependent, as were most of the other girls in the facility. One girl had been sold for sex to grown men by her mother; others had been beaten; and several had been sexually abused. Almost all had come from dysfunctional families, and had used alcohol or drugs to deal with their wounds. I used rebellion to deal with mine.

The program relied on group and individual talk therapy. The staff ate with us and played card games and pool with us. They were more like camp counselors than treatment staff.

During an individual session, I confided to one of the counselors that I'd been sexually abused. The counselor figured that a confrontation with the perpetrator would help me, so we called the family and asked them to come in for a meeting. The abuser was about twenty-two years old by then. I don't think he'd imagined that I would tell the truth, and I remember his face when I did. One moment he was grinning, the next his smile collapsed and he stood up and ran out of the room. His mother sat as still as a statue. I think she was in shock—perhaps torn between loyalty for her son and revulsion for what he'd done. The father's reaction was more overt. I can't remember exactly, but I think he called his son a bastard.

After they left, the counselors helped me to process what had happened as best they could. Years of sexual abuse, however, are not cured in months of treatment for chemical dependency. I still had a lot of healing ahead of me.

When I returned from the facility, my parents tried to impose very strict rules on me. Looking back, the restrictions were probably reasonable under the circumstances, but at the time they felt too harsh. My parents told me I could leave their house if I didn't comply. I filled a box with my clothes and bought a bus ticket to Minneapolis. I'm not sure what Hysugi and Hyogi thought about what was going on. It's all a cloudy picture in my mind now. I think they were frightened, but they didn't say anything. My brother was living somewhere else by then.

It was just before my seventeenth birthday. The bus dropped me off in St. Paul, and a girlfriend whom I'd met in treatment took me in temporarily. Another friend, Chris, was a year older than I was and living in Minneapolis. I'd met him at the treatment center, too. He'd got out months before I did. When I told him on the phone that I had left home, he offered me a place to stay. Within weeks, I was living with him in Minneapolis.

At the time, I thought Chris was my way out of a family system that didn't work for me. I thought that he wanted to help me. I now think of my relationship with him as a profound mistake. He took advantage of me when I was vulnerable. He seemed so gentle and sweet, but he soon tired of me, especially after I'd had our baby. I was disoriented and naïve; I had no idea what a healthy relationship was; I didn't think I had the right to be respected.

Eventually, I spent one long, agonizing night at the hospital, holding my dear little baby, knowing that I was going to give her up the next morning. I knew I had to give her up because it was best for her. But one of the nurses must have made a mistake by bringing her back to me in the birthing room. I wasn't supposed to see her at all. Then I wouldn't have fallen in love. After two weeks without her, I couldn't stand it. I called the social worker and told her that I'd changed my mind.

My baby hadn't been placed with a family yet, so I was allowed visits with her until I decided for sure to take her home. My heart broke every time I saw her little face, and my love for her only grew stronger with each visit. Chris agreed to visit the baby once or twice, but it was obvious that he didn't want to be a father. So I made the decision on my own. Come hell or high water, I was going to keep my baby. Since Chris wasn't interested, everything was left to me. I felt overwhelmed.

Finally, the day arrived. I went to the foster home and loaded my daughter into a car to drive her to my apartment. I was so happy. I got to lay with her and cuddle with her. I fed her. I held her and read to her. I showed her shapes and colors, and pushed her in a stroller for miles and miles, stopping to feed her and change her diapers.

Chris was hardly ever home, so I was basically living on my own. I knew immediately I'd made the wrong choice. I had no job, and was on welfare and barely scraping by. I didn't know how to be a mother, and there was no one to help me. I didn't even have a phone to call if I needed help.

I tried to avoid the apartment as much as I could. I felt so lonely and isolated. Most of my friends had abandoned me. Many of them had pressured me to abort the pregnancy, and for some strange reason they were angry that I didn't.

Most of the time, I sang to my little angel. I didn't know what else to do but sing. I often sang a popular American lullaby:

Rock-a-bye baby in the treetop,
When the wind blows the cradle will rock
When the bough breaks the cradle will fall
And down will come baby
Cradle and all.

I felt worthless and helpless. I was breaking apart and reality was crashing in. I knew that singing lullabies wasn't a substitute for good parenting.

I could see my child was starting to suffer. I'd had her for six months, and she wasn't eating enough. She rarely smiled. By then, I was spending a lot of time crying.

Finally, just as I'd been given up for adoption, I gave up my precious little flower for good. As in 1971, I found myself at the door of Lutheran Social Services, only this time, fourteen years later, on the other side of the equation. The paperwork was simple. The social worker explained in detail that I wouldn't have any rights to the baby once I signed. I signed and walked away. I have absolutely no memory of saying good-bye to my daughter that day. I don't remember how I dressed her. I don't recall the bus ride there, nor do I remember kissing her one last time. I don't even remember crying. My mind has been benevolent enough to banish those agonizing images from my memory.

Later, I wrote a letter to my baby's new parents, telling how hard it had been to give her up. The social worker made me rewrite it. "You have to make it cheerier," she said. I had named my baby Melissa. Her new parents changed her name to Suzanne. They sent me pictures for years after they adopted her. The photographs were sent through the adoption agency, so I couldn't know where they lived. I have pictures of her until she was five or six.

It wasn't until much later in my life that I realized how the sexual abuse had affected me. Both during and after that six-year period, I walked around unconscious of how badly my heart and soul had been wounded. Some of the counseling I received helped. And it helped to hear stories from other girls in treatment who'd experienced what I did, some even worse.

The first time I saw my American father cry was the day he found out what had happened to me under his roof. I think he felt responsible, and he was furious at the perpetrator. My mother was in shock. She apologized to me, even though it certainly wasn't her fault. Indeed, she's apologized several times over the years. Hyogi has since expressed her support, and I never got the chance to talk to Hysugi about any of it. My brother has never spoken to me on the subject.

When I think of my past, I imagine a child who is hit by a car so hard that her legs have been badly damaged. The doctors do what they can, but the healing is painful and takes years, and the child will never walk normally again. To this day, metaphorically speaking, I sometimes walk with a limp. However, I don't let it stop me. The abuse is something that happened to me. It is not who I am.

While I'm not Christian, I've learned a lot about forgiveness from Christ's teachings. I managed to confront my abuser without being abusive. I stood up for myself without being vindictive. I spoke the truth about how he hurt me, and let him go.

Of course, at times I look back on my turbulent teens and cringe. If I'd known what I know now, I would have handled my pain and confusion differently. But I did the best I could.

It may seem strange, but I'm most proud that I managed the most profound act of forgiveness: I healed. I undid the damage that he inflicted upon my body, heart, mind, and soul. Now I am thriving. My abuser owes me nothing because I didn't let him ruin me. His soul is free. When he meets his maker, he won't have to ask for forgiveness. He's already forgiven, because I'm whole and I am free.

Six

THE DEATH OF AN ANGEL

THE FONDEST MEMORIES I HAVE OF MY AMERICAN FAM-
ily are of my sisters and me playing near the many lakes we
visited on those summer camping trips. We searched for skipping
stones and pretty shells. We picked berries and played games. At
night, we sat around fires and made chocolate s'mores.

Hyogi was always the smartest one of the family. She studied
hard and did very well in school. She excelled at mathematics
and was almost a virtuoso at the piano. She graduated from
high school, attained a master's in business administration, and
moved to the East Coast. She married a wonderful man, and
they have a beautiful young son. She works for a telephone
company, crunching numbers, analyzing statistics, and organiz-
ing advertisements.

Of the three of us, Hysugi was the first to fly over from
Korea, as a tiny baby. Although she began as the smallest, she
grew to be the tallest of the three daughters. Her hair had a
brilliant sheen and was so dark it almost looked blue. She was
four years younger than I was, delicate and with a spirit that
radiated kindness. She was the gentlest person I ever met, and

her smile always warmed my heart. She was only nineteen when she died.

Hysugi had graduated from high school and had gone off to college. I think it was the fall of her freshman year. She traveled home to my mother and father's house for a visit. I was living in Minneapolis at the time, a ninety-minute drive away. My brother called with the news. His voice sounded strained. I knew something was wrong immediately. My heart was beating so fiercely I could hardly hear him speak.

Hysugi had taken her own life. Even though I'd noticed that sometimes she was sad, none of us had ever dreamed she'd kill herself, or knew of any reason for her to do so. To this day, we don't know. At the time, I was afraid to ask. My relationship with my parents wasn't good, and I hadn't seen Hysugi for well over a year. Now I would never see her again.

My mind went back to when I was seven years old. Hysugi and I were playing house in her room, in which almost everything was white. I played the mommy, and she played my little baby girl. We cut little pieces of rubber band and decorated them to look like bacon. Then we drew on paper to make faux eggs. I would serve her the pretend food, and she would pretend to eat it. "More, more!" she would say. She would laugh and want me to go on and on.

The funeral was a blur. People came and went, talking to me and asking me questions, but I remember hardly anything. I wasn't there, really. I was in some kind of grief-induced daze. As far as I was concerned, the funeral was a party in her honor, and she was supposed to walk through the door at any minute.

For years afterward, I was in denial that Hysugi had died. I would pretend she was away at college and that I would see her again as soon as she graduated. Sometimes, I'd cry and scream into my pillow. *It should have been me*, I thought. *I should have been the one to die.* She was too good a person to die so young. Maybe she was just too kind and gentle for this world.

I am in a large banquet hall with tables of food around me. The table nearest to me is especially large and piled high with succulent grapes, apples, oranges, and every kind of meat. My mouth waters in anticipation. I lift my hand slowly to take a piece of fruit, but all the food disappears.

Suddenly, I can see for miles and miles. I find myself standing in the midst of complete devastation, as if a nuclear bomb has wiped out everything. I sense I'm not alone and hear breathing. I run into a church, but the breathing continues to follow me. The pews are filled with empty bodies, zombie-like people with no human emotion.

Finally, I see what's chasing me. His face is so blurry that I can't quite make him out, but I notice he has the body of an animal, like a satyr. His limbs and torso become more humanlike as I run from him. His arms grow more and more muscular, and hair sprouts all over him. Eventually, I can see that he has a rope to strangle me with.

The hollow people in the church begin a low, indistinguishable chant. I try to scream, but can't. They won't help me. They simply continue humming their menacing, rhythmic mantra.

I run outside again. The destruction has changed from twisted metal and heaps of rubble to corpses with open wounds and pools of blood all over them. The horrible scene stretches for miles. I'm tempted to give up and die at the sight of it, but the creature has come back, and the urge to survive returns.

All at once, my American family is standing with me. We're holding hands and running for our lives. I hold Hysugi's hand.

Eventually, we arrive at a stream, which we have to jump across to get away. As we jump, Hysugi's hand is ripped from mine, and I find myself on the other side looking back at my little sister. The stream swells until I know she'll never be able to cross. I watch helplessly as a giant lizard chases her. She's screaming for help, and I'm screaming back to her.

Suddenly, I am in my American parents' house. My mother and father are upstairs. I'm standing at the base of the staircase, looking up. My brother comes down with a large hair dryer and brush in his hand. "Everyone's too busy to see you, Kelly," he says. "But you can stay in the little house in the backyard."

I don't know what he means by "little house in the backyard." He begins drying his hair, so I walk outside and around the back. The little house isn't much bigger than a telephone booth. It's white and the windows are covered with screens, with no panes of glass in them. I enter the house and lie on the floor. It's cold, and I cry. I feel absolutely alone.

Then I find myself back in Korea, lying in a hay shed, looking up at the clouds as they pass above me. I can feel the warmth of the sun and the soft breeze caressing my skin. I imagine the clouds shaping themselves into magical forms—animals, dolls, and smiling faces. An airplane flies overhead, and I point at it. I run from the shed crying, "A plane! A plane!" And a warm feeling comes over me.

In one form or another, I had this dream repeatedly until I was in my twenties.

Seven

I LOVE FRANCE

B RAD AND I MET ABOUT FIVE MONTHS BEFORE MY twenty-fifth birthday. A roommate of mine introduced us. My immediate impression was that he was so good-looking he must be a jerk. But when he asked me out, I discovered that he was actually quite nice. Several months after we'd begun dating, he invited me to Paris.

"I'm going to Paris," he announced. "I was going to go with someone else, but that fell through. Would you like to come with me?"

If he was trying to impress me, it worked. Other than my first five years in Korea and a trip to Canada, I'd never been out of the United States. At first I assumed he was joking, and then I realized that he was serious. I told him I'd love to go to France with him, but I was as afraid as I was excited. I'd managed to become a white-knuckle flyer. I especially hated the takeoffs and landings. Moreover, the longer the flight, the more anxious I'd get. I also couldn't speak any French. Nonetheless, I really wanted to go. I told Brad about my fear of flying, and he held my hand that first time we took off.

Soon enough, I had to pinch myself. There I was, the small-town, Minnesota girl, sipping wine in the shadow of the Eiffel Tower, sunning myself near Notre Dame Cathedral, and window-shopping on the Champs-Élysées. I fell in love with France while I was falling in love with Brad.

Paris is the kind of city where you can spend a month and still not see everything there is to see—not only the wonderful museums (the Louvre, the Orsay, the Rodin) and the fantastic restaurants, but the mesmerizing people watching from the sidewalk cafés.

At first, I was intimidated. The Parisian women are so beautiful and sophisticated. I was afraid to enter stores or to even buy anything in the outdoor markets. Even though Brad didn't speak French, I relied on him to communicate for me.

We stayed in Paris for two weeks. Brad paid for everything and showed me a wonderful time. I couldn't wait to tell Hyogi all about it when I got back home. She was happy for me.

Brad and I would return on several occasions. Each time, I always wanted to stay longer, but I was always happy to come home, too. We always stayed in the same little inn—the Hotel de Turenne in the Seventh Arrondissement near Invalides and École Militaire. Each morning, we'd stand at the front door of the hotel and one of us would randomly choose a direction to wander. We'd walk until we were tired of walking, and then we'd sit and sip wine until we were tired of sitting. If we fancied a beer in the morning, we'd have one; if we desired coffee at night, we drank it. We slept in when we wanted and didn't feel obligated to visit any of the touristy sites. The only rule was that there were no rules. They were some of the best days I've known. I was finally, truly happy again.

Those first excursions to France occurred at the time I was trying to decide what I wanted to study in college. My practical side was pushing me toward business school. I presented the dilemma to Brad. "Shut your eyes and take a deep breath," he responded. "Forget about all the 'shoulds,' and ask yourself, *what do I really want to study?*"

My answer was instantaneous: *French.* "Well then, sign up for French," Brad said. And that was my rebirth as a Francophile. Brad convinced me that I was smart enough to go to college. And, lo and behold, I found that I was.

Within months I was sitting at a small community college with a French-language textbook in front of me and a list of words to learn. I spent one year studying at the community college and then transferred to the University of Minnesota. In 1999, I graduated from the university with a bachelor's degree in European Area Studies. My last class was a correspondence course. Brad marched me to the mailbox with the final exam in my hand.

In addition to learning the language, my studies required me to immerse myself in French culture. To fulfill that requirement I entered an immersion program located in Montpellier, in the Languedoc-Roussillon region of Southern France. I couldn't believe how far I'd literally and metaphorically traveled. I'd begun my life as a Korean, speaking Korean and eating Korean food. Then I'd become an American, with everything that goes with living in the United States. Finally, I'd fallen in love with a third culture, a third people, and a third worldview. The French language saturated my dreams, and I relished the French way of life.

I lived in Montpellier for three months. I remember the day I arrived. The taxi driver picked me up at the train station and drove me down streets, up hills, and even on a highway for a while. It wasn't until a couple of days later that I discovered that my temporary home was a five-minute walk from the station.

I lived in a two-bedroom apartment with a woman named Madame Caiozzi. She rented out both of her bedrooms to students, and slept behind a curtain in the living room. I would stay with Madame for ten weeks. The thought of being away from Brad made me want to cry.

Beside Madame Caiozzi, my other housemate was a young fellow named Lars Loth from Switzerland. Lars became like a brother to me. He and I would walk down the cobblestone streets of Montpellier together. Cars weren't allowed in the center of town, where the buildings were old and beautiful. Some of the medieval streets were paved with granite, and just outside the town center was a park with a view of a Roman aqueduct.

All my classmates thought I was crazy for walking the mile to school each day, but for me it was the best part of my day. I walked past the little shops and *boulangeries*. I savored the smell of freshly baked French bread and the sound of street merchants. Often, I'd buy a baguette and sit in the park near the city center and eat lunch, trying to soak in as much of Southern France as I could.

When I finally returned to the United States, I was surprised to experience more culture shock than I'd had going to France. I was dying to see Brad again, but I missed France so much. I wanted to scream in the streets of Minneapolis that somewhere across the ocean was a simpler and more rewarding way to live.

Part Two

ANOTHER FAMILY

Eight

FIRST CONTACT

S UNDAY, SEPTEMBER 9, 2007.
I'm sitting down in front of our living-room computer and beginning to pull up my e-mails. One has Korean characters on the subject line, and I know it's been sent by my Korean family. Suddenly, I feel as if a flock of butterflies has invaded my stomach. *What will it say? Do they want money? Are they going to ask to come to America and live with me? Did they give me up because my conception and birth were unplanned and unwelcome?*

I finish with all my other e-mails. I sit for a minute and do nothing. I can't move.

Then I click the mouse. The first words from my Korean mother to me in almost four decades spread across the screen. They are translated into English.

I'm shame and humble to you and I say.

My daughter, Myonghi! We were very surprised and shed tears of joy after heard your news. For a long time, we tried go look for you, but it was not easy. As the broadcasting station's program which we sent circumstances to was finished early, we had to get in touch with another one.

Meantime we soon heard your news.

Myonghi!! With all much endeavor we couldn't search for traces to connect with you in several procedures and steps. Korea service organization and I were contacted. But I think that they understood about something.

We have been dying to see you. I want to talk to you everything but with an overflowing joy I have only tears. Myonghi, I send a letter with Korean family's pictures. There are Father and me, three sisters and two brothers. The one of two brothers had been born after you have left for America. All family in Korea want to convey a mind which is missing you. My daughter, Myonghi, I always care about you and waiting for your letter. Every day I pray.

To Myonghi

From Mother

The question that had hung over my life all those years—*Did they love me?*—is answered with two short sentences. *We have been dying to see you. I want to talk to you everything but with an overflowing joy I have only tears.*

I lay my head in my arms and let myself weep.

I call Brad and ask him to hurry home. Soon he's sitting beside me on the couch. I read the e-mail to him, and we cry together. We bring up the pictures.

One is of me in 1967, when I'm about one year old. I look like a boy, and at first I think it's a picture of someone else. I'm dressed in a collared shirt and bow tie. Over the shirt, I'm wearing a jacket with big, round buttons down the front and more buttons on the pockets. I'm also wearing a hat that doesn't fit well. My hair is cut short above my ears, and the bangs are uneven and reach down to just above the brow. I am sporting a weak smile. Behind me are three metal bars, probably a fence. The photograph is cracked and worn.

The second picture is of me, for certain. I'm on an old piece of playground equipment. I'm wearing a nice knit dress with matching leggings and hat; a white, long-sleeved turtleneck shirt; and clogs.

The third photograph is captioned: it is of my oldest sister Whasoon and me sitting together. Whasoon was born in 1956, it says. She must have been about fifteen when the picture was taken. I would have been about four. Whasoon has a slight smile on her face and friendly, slightly squinting eyes. She is wearing a white, short-sleeved dress shirt. Her hair is long and combed over to the side. She is holding me. I look very serious for being so young. I have a haircut that looks like someone put a box over my head. I'm wearing a black dress with a white shirt.

I study the other pictures of my Korean siblings, searching to see if I look like anyone.

Myongsuk, the caption reads, is the second oldest sister, born in 1958. She is eight years my senior. There's something different about our mouths; otherwise she and I could be twins. She is standing in a kitchen with a stainless-steel refrigerator, a large aluminum pot, and a white tile wall. She is waving her hand in front of her, apparently signaling that she doesn't want her picture taken at that moment.

Myongja is the next in line, born in 1962. She's sitting at a kitchen table with her chin and cheek resting in her hand. The quality of the photo is poor, but the kitchen appears to be well appointed. My family is obviously doing much better now.

There is a photograph of Chulsoo, sitting in a chair, looking stern. He has hair down to his shoulders. His face is a bit blurry, but he looks handsome, with strong features.

The youngest, Pyongsoo, also resembles me, although not as strongly. He was born in 1973, several years after I went off to America. He's a handsome young fellow with a devilish grin, long flowing hair, and a boyish face.

Finally, we open the picture of my mother and father together. My father was born in 1928, which would make him eighty. It is clear from the curtain and equipment in the background that the photograph was taken in a hospital or nursing home. He is balding and gray and looks very tired and weak. I assume he isn't well. I can see faint reflections of my siblings in his features. My mother sits next to him. Her hair is permed and dyed black, making her look years younger than my father. Although she isn't smiling, she looks content.

It feels strange to call them my family.

I'm unable to reply until days later. I want to communicate with my Korean mother, but I can't find the right words. There is too much to say. I have a thousand questions.

Finally, I'm ready. I look at the old orphanage picture of me, studying the forlorn look on my face. Then I sit at the computer and begin to type.

Mother,

I am extremely happy to hear from you and to know that the family is all doing well. Your letter was such a surprise. I have often dreamt of finding you all again, but never really thought it was going to happen.

Thank you for the pictures. I would like to send pictures of myself, husband, and children. I have a girl eight years old, and a son five years old. I will write more later, because I am overwhelmed with emotion and I need some time to think about things. Know that I am extremely happy to hear from you and wish to see you all sometime in the near future.

Does anyone in the family speak English or French? I do not speak any Korean. I have not been exposed to it since I came to America.

Sincerely,

Kelly

My Korean mother's second e-mail message, a reply to mine, comes within a week:

SATURDAY, SEPTEMBER 22, 2007

My dear Kelly,

I received your answer well.

As your answer was speedy, I'm very surprised and excited.

I wanted to write to you quickly but nobody can speak English and French. So we have to receive help from a neighbor who can speak English. Please, take in the situation.

I'm happy to receive your pictures. I was relieved to hear your pleasant life with your family in the US. I'm very thankful that you could have kind foster parents and present family. All of Korean family are delighted with your letter and pictures.

You are the perfect image of your sisters.

Although I first saw your looks after you left, you are a precious daughter. You are already an adult, however, you are a lovely young girl to me.

Well, as I was saying, we can't speak English and French. For all that I got your phone number, I can't speak to you over the telephone. I want to listen your voice, but it seems to be impossible.

So, we decided to go English institute to prepare meeting with you. Even though to communicate in English might be difficult, we'll do our best. We are anxious for meeting with you.

I send my pictures, your father's pictures and your pictures as you were young. Not much later, letters of brothers and sisters will reach after arrival of this letter.

I and your father extremely hope to meet and touch you before we die.

I hope that your business goes well. God bless you!

I love you.

With love,

Mother

Sitting alone in the living room, I notice that my hands are clenched into tight balls. My breathing is shallow and irregular. I take a breath and let out a sigh. Finally, I let go and cry.

I wonder if reading every letter from them will be this painful.

I am holding my little baby girl. She is so beautiful. I pull back the blanket to see her little feet. They are red on the bottom, so very small and vulnerable.

Her pink fingers wrap around my finger, and the grip is surprisingly strong. It's as if her little hand is asking me to stay with her. But I have so little to offer. I have no education, no job, no money, and no father for her. There is nothing at home, not even a baby blanket.

I'm nineteen years old. It's February 1986. I'm lying in the hospital bed, holding my baby and knowing I'm going to have to give her up. I look into her little eyes and feel completely empty, as if I have been gutted.

That night, I stare at the ceiling for hours. The woman on the other side of the curtain has fallen asleep, and I can hear her heavy breathing. Another baby's cries echo down the hospital corridor.

I've made such bad choices. But I can at least make one good one, one that will give my precious child a chance.

I don't want anyone to see me cry, so I lie quietly in the dark room, silently letting the tears fall onto my pillow.

The next morning I walk out of the hospital, leaving my baby behind for another family to love.

MONDAY, SEPTEMBER 24, 2007

Dear Mother,

I am writing to you with a wild range of emotions. Please know that I am extremely happy to have finally reconnected with you after 37 years, but I also have a lot of confusion about how I should proceed.

The word "ashamed" was included in your first e-mail. I may be mistaken, but I assume that you are saying that you feel bad about putting me up for adoption. If I am understanding your words correctly, I suggest that you should feel no shame. I know you did what you had to do during a very difficult time. Sometimes circumstances force one to make hard choices.

My life in America has given me opportunities I may have never had in Korea. I have had the chance to go to college, study in France and do a lot of travel abroad.

My life is good. I have a loving husband and two beautiful children. My daughter is 8 years old, and my son is 5 years old. I have been lucky to stay home with both my children. Now that

they are in school, however, I have begun working for Homeland Security at the Minneapolis airport.

It may be too soon to talk about, but I would very much
like to meet you all and to have you meet my family. I see
that father is getting up in age, and I would like to make a
visit to Korea while he is still well. If you agree to meet me
and my family (husband Brad, daughter Cecilia, and son Max),
I would like to consider traveling to Korea in the next year,
perhaps. Let me know how you feel about this. Certainly, if
you feel uncomfortable with us visiting you, I will honor your
feelings.

Love,

Kelly

Sometimes, I think, if it were up to my husband, we'd rent a
billboard to announce that I've found my biological family. His
excitement and enthusiasm often bubble over. He's sending some
videos of me to my older brother Chulsoo's e-mail address—of
me bringing my daughter to the bus on her first day of kindergarten, me demonstrating the art of making sushi, me scurrying
around the kitchen trying to avoid being filmed by Brad.

On a Saturday morning, I pull up my account to check my
e-mail. Chulsoo has written.

SATURDAY, SEPTEMBER 29, 2007
Dear Kelly,
This is from your younger brother, Chulsoo. Thanks for your
letter and videos.

Though it was a short one, you in that video are familiar

with me. Your siblings here in Korea have had many conversations about reflections in our family. We are so happy about that we shall meet . . . and think about which words will do when we meet.

We always think about you although we have shared not so many letters. Mother showed tears when she got your address and phone number. If she could speak English, she would call you and hear your voice . . . she is so sorry about that.

We all the family miss you so much. Mother shows tears when she just hears your name.

If you want to know why you were adopted, I will tell about that, but if you don't, I won't.

We study English to show and explain our heart. Please say hello to Brad. I'll send you letters as many as I can.

Sincerely,

Chulsoo.

Here I am, communicating with my little brother—the baby I remember trying to hold as he struggled to free himself from my grasp. He's all grown up now and has a family of his own. I can't believe he's an adult. Reading his letter, I feel a closeness I didn't think possible.

We receive several pictures from Chulsoo. Some are of his wife and children. One is of my entire Korean family, posing together. My father and mother are seated in the foreground, with my five siblings standing behind them. Everyone is dressed formally. The expressions on my parents' faces are solemn. Myongsuk, the second sister, is smiling. Whasoon, my oldest sister, has a mischievous grin and is looking off to the side, toward someone else in the room. My two brothers stand awkwardly with their hands clasped in front of them, two young men tolerating the occasion. Myongja, the third sister, has an expression as serious as my parents'.

The photograph must have been taken in the late eighties or early nineties because my father looks young and my youngest brother, Pyongsoo, appears to be still in his teens; Chulsoo seems to be in his early twenties.

The question continues to haunt me: *Out of six children, why was I the only one that they gave away?*

SATURDAY, OCTOBER 6, 2007

Dear Chulsoo,

Thank you for the letter. It is so nice to hear from you. Each letter I have read has brought tears. I am looking forward to seeing everyone in the near future.

I would like to know more about you and your life. Looking at the pictures, I see that you have a beautiful wife. Do you have any children? Please let me know more about you and your life.

As for father, it makes me extremely sad to see that he is sick. I would hop onto an airplane now, except that is not possible at the moment.

I would like it very much if you told me why I was adopted and the history of everything I have missed out on. There are some memories I have, which I would like to talk about. Perhaps if I learn some Korean and everyone learns some English we will be able to communicate.

It is so nice to have found all of you, and I am looking forward to meeting in person. Please say hello for me.

Love,

Kelly

Chulsoo's reply:

WEDNESDAY, OCTOBER 10, 2007

Dear Kelly,

Thanks for your letter. I see that you feel the same about this situations as we do.

I thought that you probably have lost the remembrance about your childhood, but you have not and we are happy about that.

Below this, I'll tell you why you were adopted. Only what I can tell is what I've been told. . . .

You were adopted in 1971, that was just one year after I was born. At that time we families were so poor that we could not afford just one day. We rent one room, and we nine peoples lived there together. It never rains without pouring, father was very sick then.

Mother says that there was no hope of life. The madam who owned our room persuaded our parents to adopt one of children for sake of the child. Mother felt very bad about that, and said no. But the situations were so hard to stand with that mother could not help considering . . . because she thought one of our family might die from hunger. I've been told that you were very smart and gifted, so mother wanted to make you educated well. You know, need-less to say, she did not want to make you adopted. So she could not make a decision for a long time. Maybe it was your destiny, you said you want to make your life in USA. Mother remember that you used to say, "If I go to USA, I'll make a lot of money and make our family happy."

In the end, she decided to adopt you for your happiness. You left to USA and after that we got some letters and pictures from your parents-in-law. But we could not see what the letters were telling because we didn't know English. Couples of decades have passed since that, we could get better and we started to find you. However, we couldn't find any data of your adoption. Fortunately, the data that you have sent to Korea-volunteer-organization and the data that we have sent were the same ones and we could find each other.

Mother has shown tears many times a day and missed you so much. Sometimes when our families got together, she cried out, saying your name. Although I didn't know why she cried in my childhood, but I now know her mind. I think there is no word that deserves our parents' mind. If you want to know more, I'll tell you as much as I can. And later on, I'll tell you about our siblings and their families (so many families). Before you come to Korea, I'll send all the pictures of families so that you can have knowledge of families. (27 persons in our families.) With all my heart, I wish you happy.

Chulsoo

I do want to know more. I have so many questions. I begin to speculate about what my life would have been like had I stayed in Korea. I would have had to endure more years of hardship and starving. I almost certainly wouldn't have traveled to America. I wouldn't have learned to speak English. I wouldn't have studied in France or learned to speak French. I wouldn't have met my husband, and my two beautiful children would never have been born.

Part of me is glad I was the one they picked.

Why, then, do I feel such pain?

Nine

VOICES

I AM A LITTLE GIRL STANDING IN THE DOORWAY WATCH-
ing. The kitchen is dark. It is either early morning or late in
the day. I look down and see that the hem of the young woman's skirt is worn. There are marks from the dirt floor around
the bottom of her skirt, too, because she has bent down to add
wood to the fire. Her hands are busy adding things to the dish
she's cooking.

I know now that this is a memory of Whasoon. Of all my
family members, I remember her most vividly. She was the oldest sibling. She watched over me, and often took me to the river
to do laundry. I helped her to cook and clean, and she taught
me to sew with a needle and thread.

SATURDAY, OCTOBER 29, 2007

This is from your eldest sister Whasoon with all my heart missing you.

Thanks god for your being happy. I'm so happy about finding you, my sister. Since heard that news from you, I have always thought of you. Kelly, your Korean name was Myonghi. I want to call you Myonghi, indeed.

I wish I could e-mail or call you every day, if I can speak English. It is a dream come true that we can keep in touch with each other. I am very thankful to your parent-in-law about bringing you up so great.

Myonghi—You probably can't remember that you usually sang a song. I still remember that song. I cannot help crying while I write you a letter.

It is so grateful that you look great and happy with your family over there, I feel ease about that.

I miss you so much and I hope to see you asap.

Mother, father, and all the family in here are looking forward to see you. Father is very sick. He wants to see you before he died.

I love you Myonghi.

> Lots of love and missing,
> Your eldest sister in Korea,
> Whasoon

I recall singing in Korea. I remember that songs would comfort me. I don't remember my mother, but I do remember Whasoon. I thought she was my stepmother. She probably had to sing to calm me down when I was unhappy. The thought of her singing calms me even now.

I write Whasoon back:

Dear Whasoon,

I am very touched by your letter. You know, I have memories of you, though they are very vague. Is it true that we used to wash clothes in the river together? Also, I remember our home having a fence around the yard. Was father sick when I was put up for adoption? I remember him being very sick. There are so many questions in my mind. I will save some for another letter.

Also, please send me a copy of the song that I used to sing, if possible.

I will learn Korean. Perhaps if I learn some Korean and you learn English, we will be able to communicate well. My heart is aching when I think of all of you there and me here, so far away from each other. I would like to visit you all sooner, but it is not possible at the moment. Although I can try and move the date forward if father is getting too sick.

I would like more information of you. Are you married? Do you have children? Do you work? I understand it may take some time for you to answer all my questions. I am very happy to receive your letter.

Love,

Kelly

It is December 7, 2007, and I am going to hear my Korean mother's voice for the first time since 1971. The translator sits quietly as I lean over and begin pushing the phone buttons. We are in the living room. I have pushed two chairs up to opposite sides of a piano bench. The phone is on the bench between us.

Several clicks come out of the speaker. A male voice answers. The translator greets him, and the conversation begins.

"Your brother, Chulsoo, is thanking me for being here," the translator says. "He wants to know how you are."

"I'm doing fine," I reply.

"We are all very much looking forward to seeing you," Chulsoo says via the translator. I can hear his voice perfectly. "We have all to take our vacations together so we can meet you and your family. Everyone is very excited."

"We are getting ready for Korea here," I say. "Brad and the kids are looking forward to meeting everyone, too."

"Mother would like to talk with you. Do you want to talk with her now?"

My mouth goes dry. "Yes, I want to."

"Myonghi? Myonghi?" She sounds like she is short of breath. "Thank you for talking with me. We are all missing you very much. You are my Myonghi. I never stop loving you. Thank you for not being angry, thank you for accepting letters and for calling. Do you remember me? It's OK, you were so young."

I have never remembered my mother, but I don't want to hurt her feelings. "I'm not sure if I remember you or my older sister," I say. "I get the memories mixed up."

"I want to thank your parents for being good to you," she says. "You are not angry at us, so I want to thank them for bringing you up good. Thanks to your husband. He is a very good man. I can tell he loves you very much. I want him to know we are grateful."

"Yes, I am very lucky," I answer.

"Do you remember me?" she repeats. "Do you have many memories of Korea?"

I try to remember. An image of someone holding my hand flashes through my mind. A glimpse of a skirt brushing against my cheek. A pair of shoes and another worn-out skirt. A black braid.

"Well, I'm not sure," I say. "I have memories, but I don't know whether they're of you or not."

"Of course, I don't expect you to remember me. You were so young when you left. You were just a baby, four years old."

She starts to cry. I begin to cry, too.

"You know, I love you very much," she says. "It was so hard to give you up. We were very poor and could not feed everyone. I was told you . . ." She sighs and takes a couple of breaths before she can go on. "You have a better life in the United States. There were too many mouths to feed. We were hardly able to feed the family. You were so smart and happily wanted to go to U.S., to get enough to eat and to make lots of money. You would say, 'I make lots of money and I get airplane and fly you all to America.'"

I remember lying in the hay shed, looking up at the sky, watching the clouds, and pointing at the planes as they flew above me. "I haven't made enough to buy that airplane," I say, "but I'm getting enough to eat."

She laughs, and then there is a moment of silence.

"We search and search for you," she says, "but nobody knows where you are. The orphanage said you live with a family in Minneapolis, but then you disappear. It takes so long to find you again. I always loved you."

"It's OK, Mother. I have had a good life, and I am happy with a good husband and wonderful kids."

I am trying to be kind, but it only makes her feel worse. She begins to weep. She cries so hard that she's losing her breath.

Chulsoo takes the phone.

"Mother has left the room," he says. "She is too sad and crying very hard in the other room now."

I can hear her sobbing in the background. "Is she OK?" I ask.

"She is fine. It has taken so long to find you. Now we have found you and there is much joy, she is crying for her lost little girl. Now she has found her big girl. Whasoon would like to talk with you now."

"Yes."

"Hello, Myonghi. This is your oldest sister, Whasoon. We are all happy to have found you."

"I'm happy to be found. It's because of my husband, Brad. He wrote a letter to the social service."

"Yes, yes. We want to thank Brad very much for loving you so much," she says. "Do you remember me?"

I can see the sun and the water. I am jumping from rock to rock while my sisters wash clothes. They let me help. I rub the clothes on a rock. My sister's young hands are in the water.

"Yes, I think I do. I remember you washing clothes down by the river while I played nearby. I can also remember cooking over a fire."

"You used to come to the river with me when I had to wash. I took care of you most of the time. Did you know that? And eggs were your favorite food. You loved eggs so much. And you were a good singer. You loved to sing."

"What about Grandpa?" I ask. "Did he live with us?"

"Yes, he lived with us for a while before he died; Grandma, too. Do you know why you were taken to United States? We were so poor, Myonghi. There was never enough to eat. When the landlady came to get the rent, she would tell Mother she had too many mouths to feed. She would tell Mother to give up one of her children for a better life and fewer mouths to feed. Mother didn't want to do it. But she realized how poor we were and how hard it was to feed everyone. She and Father were always gone working to try and get enough money to feed us."

"Yes," I say. "Chulsoo told me in one of his letters that we were very poor and it was difficult for Mother to give me up."

"We prepared you. Mother felt you had the most hope. You were so smart and friendly. You were not afraid of anything or anyone. When we told you what America would be like, you were excited to go. You used to hug Chulsoo and say, *My baby brother*. He would start crying, but you still wanted to carry him around."

I remember trying to pick up my little brother. He fussed because he wanted to walk on his own.

"I can remember wanting to hold Chulsoo," I say. "And I remember praying to Buddha when I came. Was I Buddhist? My mom here tells me that I also knew about Jesus. She had a little botanical bowl with plants growing in it with a golden Buddha in the middle. I prayed to Buddha every night before bed. She let me do this for as long as I wanted, but she also took me to church every Sunday."

"A lot of Koreans are now becoming Christians," she responds. "Most are changing and some go to both."

"That's what I have heard."

"We are so grateful and happy to contact you again," Whasoon adds. "We are very much looking forward to seeing you, touching you. Mother and Father want to see you very much, Father before he dies."

She begins to cry. I begin to cry, too.

"Korea is very different now," Whasoon continues. "It is much nicer than when you were here. We are not poor and the country is not poor anymore."

"I remember Grandpa cutting the head off a chicken. Do you remember that, too? Was there a tree stump in our yard?"

"Yes," she says. She begins to cry again. "You know we all love you much, Myonghi. We're so glad we found you."

"We're glad, too," I say.

Neither of us wants to hang up, but we both sense it is time to end the conversation.

"Good-bye," Whasoon says.

"Good-bye."

There is a second or two of delay, and then some fumbling with the receiver on the other end. There is a click, and it's over.

My son and daughter come up from the basement, where they've been playing. Brad enters the room with them.

"Hey, guys," Brad says, "something big happened up here while you were playing. Mom just talked to her brother, sister, and mother for the first time in thirty-seven-years."

My daughter tilts her head to the side a bit. "Can we watch a movie?" she asks.

Ten

LEARNING KOREAN

I SPOKE FLUENT KOREAN WHEN I ARRIVED IN 1971, BUT
other than a few words I have completely lost it. In elementary school my ability to speak Korean evaporated in less than a
year. I still remember that *piapa* means "stomachache" and *koegee* means "meat," and I know a few other words, but that is all.

Now that I'm in my forties, the few words I recall will not be
of much help when we land in Incheon. It's a common miscon-
ception that the brain saves unused language like some cranial
cistern, and that once it's opened, it all comes rushing back.
There is no Korean space in my head waiting to be tapped.

I can't speak Korean now largely because I didn't want to
when I was small. I wanted to be like all the other American
kids. Anything Korean was something I wanted to forget or
leave behind.

Of course, my physical appearance is something that can't be
changed. I remember wondering why I had such dark hair, dark
skin, and different eyes and nose. I had to wear sunglasses on
my cheeks because I had no bridge on my nose like the other
children.

I have a book and a CD that will supposedly teach me to speak Korean, and Brad has three Korean dictionaries from a used bookstore. But I haven't used any of them. Brad, however, is learning more Korean than I am. He's diligent and dedicated. I tell myself that I never have the time to sit down and study, but I'm beginning to realize, in fact, that I'm afraid. That fear might be caused by the old childhood feeling that I should forget or suppress anything Korean; or maybe my former language is a gateway to my past experience and all of the painful emotions that go with it.

Still, Korea has always been in my heart. When we were watching one of the Summer Olympics on television years ago, the Korean men's swimming team won a relay. Four Korean men were hugging each other and celebrating. Brad turned to me and asked if I felt solidarity with them, if I thought of myself as one of them. It was strange, and I felt a bit guilty for saying it, but I had to answer that I did. I was an American, but I felt joy because the Korean team had won. I guess you can take the girl out of Korea, but you can't take Korea out of the girl.

In addition to relearning some of the Korean language, I am trying to regain some knowledge of Korean culture. In particular, Brad and I are learning Korean etiquette. We hired a young Korean man from the university to teach us, among other things, what behaviors to avoid so we don't offend anyone in Korea. We don't want to be the "ugly Americans." We're very sad that some of our countrymen give all Americans a bad name, and we'll do everything we can to represent our country well.

We learn that it is customary in Korea to wait for the eldest person at the table to begin eating before you do. It's very offensive to blow your nose at the table. And if you wish to fill your glass, you should first fill the glass of the elder seated next to you, using both hands.

We also discover that it is common practice for Koreans to minimize. For instance, instead of asking for a glass of water when you're thirsty, you ask for a little water. You'll still be given a full glass. It's simply considered more polite to stipulate that you don't really want much. I can already tell that my husband will struggle with this. He's used to asking for exactly what he wants.

The list of prohibitions is daunting. You shouldn't write someone's name in red ink because it signifies that they're dead. You shouldn't stab your rice with chopsticks and leave them stuck in it; this also indicates that someone has died. You shouldn't point at people with your index finger, or signal someone to come over with your hand palm-up and fingers gesturing. You shouldn't touch someone's leg to get their attention when you sit next to them. When you visit, you should bring gifts, though not expensive ones, and they should be wrapped in specific colors of wrapping paper. When you give a gift, it's best to present it with both hands. If you have to use one hand, use the right; *never* offer a gift with only the left hand.

I'm learning about Korea from other sources, as well. I speak to a Filipina about the status of women in Korea. She immigrated to Korea when she was in her twenties as a "mail-order" bride and eventually had two daughters with her husband. He was then killed in a car crash. She supports the girls by teaching English to Koreans. She and the two girls share a one-bedroom apartment in an urban high rise. Korean women, she claims, are starting to avoid marriage. Many now work outside their homes, but domestic chores and child care are still considered woman's work. Consequently, according to her, many women opt to stay single or marry foreign men. The Korean birthrate has dropped to one of the lowest in the world. Indeed, it's now so low that the government is considering immigration reform to bolster the shrinking workforce.

I learn that although the status of Korean women has improved, they've still got some way to go. They didn't win suffrage until 1948 with the writing of the Republic's new constitution. That was thirty years after the U.S. Constitution was amended to give American women the same right.

Talking to that Filipina reminds me of something that happened some years back. We were in a Vietnamese restaurant near our home in Minneapolis, and a man asked Brad how much he paid for me. He saw an American man with an Asian wife and assumed I'd been purchased. Brad laughed at first because he thought the man was joking, but the man wasn't. I was deeply offended. Since then, I've seen several online ads for Asian mail-order brides.

Eleven

PREPARING FOR THE JOURNEY

B RAD AND I WATCH AS CECILIA (OR CICI, AS WE CALL
her) and Max pack their little bags. Max wants to know if he
should bring a raincoat and umbrella. Cici wants to know how
many dresses she should pack, and if it will be uncomfortable
meeting the Korean family.

"There will be a lot of adults running around crying," Brad
says. "Mom will be crying, too."

"Will you cry, Dad?" Cici asks.

"Probably. But do you guys know what your job is?"

"What?"

"Your job is to be kids. You can give Mom a hug or rub her
back a little bit, but it's not your job to take care of her."

"Whose job is it?" Max chimes in.

"Mine," Brad says.

Brad has made a flowchart of the photos that were e-mailed
to us so we can connect faces with names. We have notified the
American consulate of our itinerary in case Kim Jung Il and the

North Korean army decide to invade while we're there. (This isn't required, but the American government suggests it because of the political tensions between the U.S. and North Korea.) We've bought movies to keep the kids occupied on the flight over. And we're trying to eat at all the local Korean restaurants so we can become familiar with Korean food.

The Twin Cities restaurant that seems to have the best and most authentic Korean food is a little place in St. Paul, Minneapolis' sister city. Its name is Mirror of Korea, and we eat there hoping the kids will have enough fermented vegetables, soups, and stews so they don't flip out when my Korean family feeds them. The owner's name is Ohk, a sweet Korean woman with an intense love for children.

We start with several different kinds of stews. Most look different than any American stews I've ever seen, but taste quite good. One is a fish stew with vegetables, rice dumplings, and a white broth. It tastes fine—like fish with onions, although I don't like the fish skin and bones that are part of it. Another dish, however, has spicy fish, and is delicious. We eat a wonderful soup that consists of tofu, potatoes, onions, and lots of bean sprouts. Then there is the clam soup, which has white creamy broth with vegetables and clams galore. The smell is enticing, and the soup has a strong, fishy taste, which I enjoy immensely, until it becomes too much for my Americanized taste buds. We devour many of the delicious side dishes. I especially love Ohk's spicy pork.

Brad likes *bibimbap*—a conglomeration of rice, beef, vegetables, and egg, stirred together in a bowl. He doesn't, however, like the soups.

We decide to present a photograph album with a large collection of pictures for my parents and a smaller version for each of my siblings. As a result, we fill six albums with pictures of my

American life. I look through my childhood photos and pick out the ones I like best. Brad stays up half the night printing and arranging photos.

I look at the first picture of me taken in America. I am five-and-a-half. It's December 1971. I'm sitting in an airport lounge chair, wearing a gray sweater with a pattern of black-and-white stripes across my chest. My adoptive mother has her arm around me. My new baby sister is in her lap. My American brother is standing in the foreground, smiling. It's three a.m., and I look confused and very frightened.

I vaguely remember getting off the plane on that cold morning. All sorts of adults were milling about, tall bodies all around me, like I was entering a moving forest.

I e-mail Chulsoo and ask for pictures of my Korean grandfather, because I have such fond memories of him. But there's a mix-up in the translation, because I receive only pictures of my Korean father. One photograph is of my father with another man, possibly my uncle. Both men wear Western suits and ties. They stand near a pile of freshly turned dirt and what appears to be an open grave. My father straddles a coil of wire, with one foot firmly planted on a flat, rectangular stone—a gravestone, I assume. My uncle stands with both feet on the same stone.

Both men carry framed pictures. My father holds an image of an old man; my uncle a portrait of an old woman. The details are hard to make out, but I assume the portraits are of my grandparents. The accompanying e-mail says the photograph was taken at the funeral of my grandfather. The two sons seem to be honoring their parents by holding portraits of them near the grave.

The next morning, I walk into the dining room and see two new pictures on the table. I recognize them immediately. They are the same pictures my father and his brother held at the gravesite. Brad took the time to crop them, blow them up, and sharpen the images.

I look more closely at what I presume to be my grandfather. I see a man with a small oval face wearing a crown-shaped hat. A Fu Manchu mustache and beard obscure his mouth. The look on his face is serious, not the smiling one I remember. The ears seem big and stick out noticeably, like mine. I don't see any other resemblance to me. This is supposedly the man I remember being so kind to me—yet now I don't recognize him.

In my saddest moments as a child, when I felt lonely and unloved, I thought about my grandfather's love for me. I remember his hand wrapped around mine. I remember him cutting the head off a chicken in our yard to feed us all. I remember crawling across the floor one night, while he was sleeping, to check his mouth for food. And I remember him lying ill in our dim room. He coughed from time to time, and was hardly able to sit up. He was already sick before I left.

My adopted mother told me that when I first came to the States, I used to say *Harabuzhi*. Then, because I couldn't speak English yet, I would lie down on the living room carpet, stiff as a board. Then I'd make an exaggerated motion by raising my hand to my mouth and I would cough. By acting out this drama, I was trying to tell her that my Korean grandfather was sick.

My grandmother's picture is easier to make out: the quality of the image is much better. Nonetheless, her face is not familiar, either. She looks like an American Indian. Her nose is wider than those of the rest of my Korean family, but her eyes are narrower. Her head is wider and more square. She is wearing a traditional Korean woman's robe and sash.

Another photo Chulsoo has sent me is of my father when he was in his early twenties, in about 1950, near the start of the civil war. He is a straight-backed, proud young man with a strong jaw. He wears a gray suit jacket, a sweater, a dress shirt, a tie, and tennis shoes. He stands in front of a pond, with a bridge in the background. The low shadows in the background suggest that it is either early morning or late afternoon. His expression is perplexed and vacant at the same time.

The picture of my parents' wedding is a surprise. I expect my mother to be wearing a traditional Korean wedding dress, but she wears a Western one. She looks quite elegant, with her hair up and adorned with flowers. A long lace train gathers at her feet. Both she and my father wear white gloves. The wall behind them is painted with a forest scene, complete with two beautiful swans. There are two potted plants behind them, and two panels with Asian characters on scrolls. Both my parents look very young.

My favorite photo is that of a birthday celebration for my father. He looks to be in his late sixties. There are several children's faces, and a man watching my father and mother. My mother is helping my father blow out the candles on his cake. She appears to be suppressing a smile. *What are they saying to each other? Are they thinking of me while they are gathered together? Do they miss me?* My heart pounds just a bit harder. A dull pain develops in my chest.

The cake is huge: three tiers with frosted flowers and baby's breath. Two massive candles are on top, one blue and one red, and several smaller, white candles, too. Several of the candle flames are flickering, with just a bit of smoke rising up.

I wonder what it will be like to be in Korea, laughing and celebrating with them.

Twelve

MY HUSBAND AND CHILDREN

WHEN MY KOREAN FAMILY ASKS ME ABOUT MY LIFE, I'M not sure where I'll begin. It's been thirty-seven years, and so much has happened. I'm relatively confident that they'll like my husband. He's friendly and enjoys meeting people. He was a freaky, uptown hairdresser with blond curls down to the middle of his back when I met him. He had earrings and even some braids with beads. He was so wild-looking. His eyes were an even more intense blue than they are now.

He and I fought a lot when we were first together. He can be a bit of a control freak, and it's atypical for him to acknowledge he's ever wrong about anything. I can be a bit of a defeatist and victim at times. But we worked it out. He's a good husband, and I love him. I'm happier now than I've ever been.

Brad proposed to me during one of our trips to Paris, on the Champ de Mars, just yards from the Eiffel Tower. When he pulled out the ring box, I thought, *Have you been going into my jewelry box?* He opened it, and I realized that he wanted to marry me. I cried. We hugged, and then went to our favorite restaurant in Paris, a little Vietnamese place called Les Trois Sequiem, right off the Rue Cler.

We were married in the living room of our house not much later. The judge who conducted the ceremony was a mountain of a man with a long, gray beard. There were only twenty guests. Lars, my schoolmate in Montpellier, came all the way from Switzerland for the occasion.

Brad is my soul mate. He's helped me to understand and work through my past. I wouldn't have grown emotionally as much as I have without him. He's given me strength beyond any other person. I thank my lucky stars that he came into my life.

Cici was born in 1999. I was sleeping in bed when my water broke early in the morning of May 21st. We went straight to the hospital, but the medical staff sent us back home, telling us not to come back until the labor pains were one minute apart. I sat on the front porch of our house for the better part of the day. Brad alerted the neighbors, and they had a "labor party" in the front yard in my honor. I endured the labor while everyone else had a great time!

When we finally returned to the hospital, I was sent straight into the birthing room. The nurse examined me and determined that Cici was just about to come out. The doctor entered, socialized with the staff, and put on his gloves and smock. When he examined me, though, his smile immediately soured. He whispered something to the nurse, and she shot out of the room. Nurses and doctors started running in with all sorts of equipment. A large man, whom I assumed was a surgeon, rushed in with surgical gloves on and his hands in the air, ready to operate. Apparently, Cici was a breech baby. She was coming out folded in half, butt first.

It was a horribly painful birth. I'd refused anesthetic until the last minute, and it was too late to medicate me once they figured out Cici was a breech. Luckily, the doctor was very experienced, and removed her without surgery. She emerged with her head perfectly formed and eyes wide open. The first person she saw was Brad. Her eyes are brown now, but they were an intense aqua blue for all of her first week.

Max was born two years later on February 15th. I was 105 pounds when we conceived him, and he tipped the scale at 9.6 pounds. All the nurses stopped by to see the little Asian woman who had given birth to the largest baby on the ward.

Max's first year was a nightmare, and we thought he wasn't going to live through it. His intestines bled profusely, and he was in immense pain a lot of the time, especially during the night. Brad had to work, so I took on most of the responsibility of comforting Max while he screamed at the top of his lungs and writhed in agony. We were so exhausted that I thought Brad and I were going to collapse. The hospitals let us down when it came to Max's sickness. They just kept sending us home, telling us to be patient and that whatever ailment it was would work itself out. Finally, one of Brad's friends told us about an over-the-counter medicine for infants. Brad bought it, and Max recovered immediately. All of those sleepless nights had been unnecessary.

Max had two surgeries his first year, as well. Infant boys' testicles have to drop down from their bodies. One of Max's didn't, and the first surgery corrected that. The second surgery was to put tubes in his ears because of repeated infections. He lost some hearing in both ears, probably from the infection fevers. He wears hearing aids now. Otherwise, he's perfectly healthy and normal.

I was lucky enough to stay at home with my children until Max was five. I work full-time now—early mornings and weekends—and Brad works nights and Saturdays. Brad's mother watches the children on Saturdays, so we can both go to work.

Brad and I don't spend enough time together, but we both agree that the children are the priority right now. Childhood passes so quickly.

I can't imagine what life was like before I was married and my children were born. I don't remember what I did with my time. Now I am Cici's mom, or Max's mom. That is my identity, and I love it.

Part Three

RETURN

Thirteen

TOUCHING THEM AGAIN

S OMETIMES, I FEEL SO EXCITED ABOUT REUNITING WITH my family that I can hardly breathe. Other times I want to cancel the Korea trip, pay the extra airline fees, and go to Paris for two weeks. I catch myself holding my breath, and the tightness in my chest and shoulders can become so intense that I think I might pull a muscle. The questions begin to run through my head. *What if that flight attendant hadn't switched my sweater with Hyogi's? Would they have found me sooner? What would my life have been like if I'd grown up in Korea? Will I like my family? Will they like me?*

During the last few weeks there have been massive protests in Seoul. One *New York Times* front-page photo showed an intersection in downtown Seoul with thousands of people marching. Over 35,000 people took to the streets to protest the lifting of a ban on American beef imports that had been in place for the last five years. Thousands of riot police were deployed. While I will blend in, Brad and the kids are obviously American. Will they be safe in Seoul?

What I'm most afraid of is what my Korean family will think

of me. Will they think I'm smart enough or pretty enough? They sent me to the land of opportunity, so they might wonder, *Has she accomplished enough? Is she successful enough?*

What if they don't like my husband and my kids? What if we don't fit in? What if we're too rude for them?

Most of all, I'm terrified that I will disappoint them.

Our flight leaves on Tuesday, July 15, 2008, and we return on Wednesday, July 30. On good days, I'm eager and excited, but more news coming out of the Korean peninsula makes me jittery. A South Korean tourist has been shot dead by North Korean soldiers, straining the fragile détente between the two governments. The woman, a fifty-three-year-old wife and mother, was visiting Mount Geumgang, a tourist area that Pyongyang had opened to tourism in 1998 as a goodwill gesture. She had wandered into a restricted area and ran when the North Korean soldiers confronted her. They shot her twice in the back. She died instantly.

The South Korean government issued a protest, suspended all tours to the Mount Geumgang resort, and demanded that Pyongyang allow an investigative team from the South to conduct a full inquiry. Pyongyang responded by saying that the South was responsible and that Seoul should apologize for its "intolerable insult" of suspending tours to the resort.

It's been fifty-five years since the civil war ended, and my people are still killing each other.

My Korean family e-mails us a list of what they've planned for us during our two weeks in Korea:

JULY 11, 2008

Hi Kelly and Brad,

We have only one week to see each other. We are so excited. We can't wait for you to come to Korea. We have been thinking what your family wants to do in Korea. Of course, the most important thing is that you will be happy when you stay here.

Here is our plan in Korea:

17th–18th: Visiting Geumsan Mountain.

19th: Water spa and hiking.

20th: Climbing Seol Ak Mountain, which is not that hard.

21st: Visiting the seashore at Dong Hae.

22nd: Back to Geumsan.

23rd–25th: Visiting relatives' houses and Seoul.

26th–27th: Visiting to Dae Cheon Beach.

We do not think you are able to see Korean family many times. It is hot in Korea now, so we suggest you wear shorts.

Your sister's son is good at chess. We hope Max likes him.

We hope you enjoy safe trips,

Your family

Because of the time it takes to fly to Korea, we won't be landing in the country until the seventeenth. That means the entire trip is planned and scripted. I picture us being sent around on a tourist bus while my family sits in Geumsan waiting. I'm not going on this trip to see Korea. I am going home to meet and spend time with my family.

I know that I will be standing on Korean soil before my e-mail can be translated and read, but I send it anyway:

JULY 12, 2008

Dear Family,

Thanks for taking the time to plan so many things for us to do. You have obviously put a lot of time and effort into our visit. But it is not necessary for you to take us all over the place. I am coming to see the family. I don't want to cause any stress while we are there. It would be more than enough to see Seoul and go hiking one day. We are very, very excited to see all of you. We want to spend some time with everyone.

Love,

Kelly

I can't believe how scattered I am as I lead my family through airport security. Even though I work for the Transportation and Safety Administration as a security officer, I have the kids' DVD player in one of the backpacks, and I'm trying to get a sixteen-ounce tube of sunscreen through in one of the carry-ons.

"Could you step aside, please?" the security woman says.

Brad scowls at me for an instant, then softens.

"Oh, I can't believe that I left those things in there. I work here, and I know better."

She's heard a billion excuses. She flashes a faux smile and continues searching my bag.

"Mom," Cici says, "what did you do?"

"Nothing, honey. Just stand with Dad."

Just then Pat, one of my Homeland Security colleagues, recognizes me.

"Kelly, hi," she says. "What's going on?"

"I can't believe it," I say. "I went through this bag ten times, but somehow I left a sixteen-ounce tube of cream in it."

I feel foolish talking to one colleague while another rips my bag apart.

"Where are you going?" Pat asks.

"Korea." If I try to explain the whole adoption thing I'll really get flustered, so I skip it.

"Well, have a good trip."

"Thanks."

The screener finishes searching my bag. "Here's your bag. We have to keep the sunscreen. Have a nice flight."

I so want to say, "I'm nervous as hell because I am going to meet my family for the first time in thirty-seven-years. I'm nervous as hell, and I really don't give a rat's ass about the sunscreen." But I just smile, grab my bag, and head toward the gate with my husband and kids.

Fifteen hours later, I'm standing near a baggage carousel in Korea. I've never been surrounded by so many Koreans in my adult life. I think back to the time I wanted to erase my Koreanness, and I regret it. One woman turns to me and asks me something in Korean. I simply smile and shrug, apologizing in English for not speaking Korean. She smiles, bows, and goes on her way. Thirty-seven-years ago I would have known what she said.

Korea doesn't look anything like I remember. This is the cleanest and most beautiful airport I've ever been in. I'd heard that Korea had made major economic progress since the 1970s, but this level of development is far greater than I'd imagined.

Brad and the kids retrieve the bags. I position myself in front of an etched glass wall that has two sliding doors. My family is on the other side of those doors.

For the longest five minutes in my life, I stand with the carry-on bags while Brad is with the kids, waiting for the airline to cough up our luggage. I turn once or twice when the doors slide open and catch glimpses of the crowd behind me. *Will I recognize my family from the photos? Will they recognize me?* Then I look toward Brad and the kids again.

In a few moments, I will have what I'd prayed for when I was a girl. Some invisible hand is twisting my insides. *What the hell am I doing here?* My mind turns back to the orphanage. I can actually feel the hunger again. I can smell those horrible, musty vitamins. I remember longing for my family to come and take me home. I feel the desire to have my father rescue me again, to take my hand again. Thirty-seven-years later and I'm feeling all of it.

Finally, our bags pop out. Brad lifts them off the carousel. He and the kids load a cart and wheel it up to me.

"Are you ready?" Brad asks.

"Yes," I reply.

We head toward the glass doors.

We emerge as if we are on the red carpet at the Oscars, but the crowd looks past us. No one knows us. There is a moment or two of hesitation. I turn left and take a step.

Suddenly, I can see someone holding a sign: *Max and Cici.* It's one of my sisters, Myongja. I recognize her face from the photos.

And then I hear Whasoon's voice in person for the first time in nearly four decades. She shrieks with joy. She runs to me with her arms open wide.

She squeezes me so tightly I think I might be crushed. She is weeping. Then she holds me at arm's length to get a look at my face. She touches my cheeks and pushes my hair back. I barely remember this woman, but instantly love her so dearly.

Then I feel Myongja throw her arms around the two of us. I hug both of them and caress their faces. We push apart to see each other, only to throw ourselves together again.

They are both talking a mile a minute, and I don't understand a word. But I know exactly what they mean. They missed me terribly. I try to respond, but I can't even whisper. It doesn't matter.

Suddenly, I see my brother, Chulsoo, standing with his arms crossed and a big grin on his face. He is dutifully hanging back, letting his sisters enjoy the moment. I break away and give him a big hug. He reciprocates, grinning and nodding. He is so handsome, with his wavy hair and chiseled face.

I see my nephew, Sungsoo, as well. I hug him. I can't believe that I come from such a good-looking family.

Brad is fighting back tears and doing a poor job of it. He pulls himself together and starts shaking hands and introducing himself.

Cici and Max are a bit confused by it all. They're being hugged and kissed and caressed by people they can't understand and have never met. A pretty, eighteen-year-old woman steps forward. In English, she introduces herself as Sae Nu Ri Yun. She will travel with us for most of our trip and be our translator. A young man with bleach-blond hair is translating, as well, and I suddenly realize that another man has a camera pointed at me. These are a crew from the Korean Broadcasting System, and they ask permission to film the reunion and to follow us around for the trip. They want to make a documentary.

The cameras and the KBS crew are just one more part of this surreal dream. I'm meeting my family for the first time in thirty-seven-years, and it's being recorded for the whole country to share. I don't know if I should laugh or cry.

Nu Ri smiles and says, "You can call me Samantha."

"Do you mind if I cut it short to 'Sam'?" Brad asks.

She laughs. "'Sam' will be fine. I'm used to people struggling with my name. Even Koreans have trouble remembering it."

Sam is Korean-born but was raised and schooled in China. Her English is flawless.

Whasoon starts to speak, and Sam translates for her.

"We never quit looking for you," she says. "We are so happy to see you and touch you. This is like a dream. I can't believe you are here."

Chulsoo politely motions for us all to follow him. We make our way outside, toward a row of buses that has formed in a line along the curb. Whasoon and I walk arm in arm in front of the others. Brad is behind us. Up ahead Myongja and Sungsoo carefully usher my children across the street toward the first bus.

I spend the hours-long bus ride sitting with my sisters and holding their hands. Buddhist or Christian, it makes no difference. There is a God, and that God is smiling down on me. My siblings are right next to me on either side, touching me. They're real. I can feel the warmth of their bodies. I can practically feel the pulse of their hearts with my hands, their breath when they talk. It's been thirty-seven-years, and I'm back. We're together again.

We reminisce about the walled house we lived in and chickens being slaughtered on a stump in the yard. Myongja tells me that she and I didn't get along. "We used to pull each other's hair and fight," she says, laughing and putting her hands up like a boxer.

I laugh, too, and reply that I don't remember fighting with her. We compare hands, and I ask them about my deformed little finger. I recall someone stepping on it once when I bent down to pick something up. The nail is still bent and twisted. Whasoon doesn't remember.

Sam stands in the aisle of the bus, hanging on to the rail and trying to keep up with translating for three reunited sisters. Max looks out of the window, watching the Korean countryside pass by. Cici is fighting off jet lag, while Brad strains his neck, trying to take it all in, looking back at me and my rediscovered treasure.

Two hours later I find myself on a sidewalk in Daejon, a city of over a million people. It's a busy sidewalk on a busy street.

Brad, the kids, and I have gotten off the bus. Whasoon and Myongja are introducing us to the nephews and nieces. There must be twenty of them, all with welcoming smiles and impeccable manners. Max and Cici are reserved at first. Then they start playing with the young Korean kids as if they've always known one another.

Korean strangers pass by and look at us curiously, trying to figure out what all the smiles, tears, and hugging are about.

Suddenly a car pulls up and a woman hops out. It is Myongsuk, my other sister. The crowd parts for her, and she walks to me and falls into my arms.

We hold each other for a few seconds, then step back to look at each other. She is eight years older, but we could be twins. "It's been a long time," she says.

"Yes it has," I reply.

She reaches back and pulls two young men out of the crowd. "These are my boys."

They are two young, sturdy-looking Korean men.

"They're both very handsome," I say.

She smiles and bows.

"Those are my children." I point to Max and Cici, who are ripping around with the younger kids.

"Very nice," she says.

"You remind me of me," I say. The likeness between the two of us is almost scary. She smiles and nods.

"Chulsoo doesn't want to rush you," Sam interjects, "but we have to get going to Geumsan, where your mother lives."

Everyone piles into vans and cars, and off we go again.

⁂

I fall asleep on the ride from Daejon to Geumsan. I don't want to be rude, but my eyelids feel like little lead curtains. I wake up when the car stops.

I can see three or four people standing around an elderly woman. She is sitting in what looks like an aluminum wheelchair.

Brad hops out of the car. "Kelly, there's your mother!" He recognizes her from the pictures.

The shock of seeing my mother sweeps the cobwebs of sleep from my brain. I hesitate for a moment, then get out of the car and walk over to her. She wails my name and begins to weep before I touch her. "Myonghi-ya! Myonghi-ya!"

My mother's wheelchair is actually a walker with a seat. She stands up and pulls me close with all of her strength, crying my name over and over. I am awestruck because I'm standing here holding my Korean mother after so many years.

She wears a white linen shirt with green slacks. Her hair is nicely styled, and she has glasses. The hard years have bent her spine, but her voice is strong and her eyes are bright. She is talking excitedly in Korean. I can't understand any of it.

I don't know what to say to her. I feel like I'm watching a foreign movie, but somehow my image has been transposed onto the screen.

Sam finally emerges from the car and starts translating. A woman standing next to my mother speaks, while my mother wipes her cheeks and tries to pull herself together.

"I'm one of your mother's friends," she says via Sam. "I

remember you when you were just a little girl. I used to see you when I came over to visit."

"It's nice to meet you," I say.

"Your mother always cried because she missed you so much."

I smile and nod.

My mother is still crying, "This is my baby! My baby! My baby!" She keeps patting my hand and looking into my face.

The memories should come flooding back now. My body was formed inside this woman. I should know her. Her face should come back to me, the sound of her voice, her eyes. I smell the subtle aroma of an unfamiliar perfume. She strokes my face and cries my name over and over again. Her heart has been broken because she gave up her little girl all those years ago. But I don't remember her, and that's what breaks my heart. I want to remember, but there's nothing.

She repeats something else in Korean. For some reason, Sam doesn't translate the rest of it.

A handsome young man stands next to my mother. I realize that he's my youngest brother, Pyongsoo, who was born several years after I left for America.

"Hello, Pyongsoo."

He bows, smiles, and says something to Sam.

"Your brother says that it's good to finally meet you. He's heard a lot about you."

I laugh and say, "I'm sure you have." The lighthearted moment is a welcome relief.

My mother finally motions for all of us to move down the walk toward the house. We all walk slowly, letting her go ahead with her walker. I can't be sure whether she is moving slowly out of emotional or physical pain.

Her house is a sturdy single-story, redbrick structure with a flat roof. It looks relatively new, probably built in the eighties.

The front yard is a walled garden with scallions growing, something that looks like wild arugula, and another vegetable that appears to be zucchini or cucumber.

Sam instructs us that it is important to take our shoes off at the door. We do. Soon twenty pairs of shoes are spread out in the front foyer.

Sunbok, Chulsoo's wife, is the first to greet us when we enter. She holds her baby boy in her arms, and her one-year-old daughter clings to her thigh. "Welcome," she says in English.

"Ah, you know English," I reply.

"Very little." She holds up her hand with the thumb and fore-finger an inch apart.

For the next few minutes I bow and shake hands, meeting all the people already in the house. I'm not sure who's who. Some are extended family. Some appear to be friends.

A chair has been placed right next to the door, and several of my family members gesture for me to notice who is sitting in it. It's an old man. He's nicely dressed in a short-sleeved dress shirt and dress slacks. Sam explains that the family brought him from the nursing home to meet me. His thin forearms are covered with bruises from the needles the doctors have used to save him from his recent sickness. He is my father.

He looks into my eyes for a moment, then turns them down and away. I kneel down and take his hand. He looks repeatedly at me and then away, saying nothing.

Whasoon and my mother sit on either side of him, speaking emphatically in Korean. I can hear my Korean name repeated several times.

I look at him carefully and try to remember his face. But his features don't seem familiar. He doesn't seem to recognize me, either.

I feel incredibly sad inside. A hollow, primal sigh rises from inside of me, but I try to suppress it the best I can. It's no use. This is the person I had prayed for day after day when I was a little girl; the man who should have come to save me. This moment is one of the biggest disappointments of my life.

"Hello, Father," I say.

He doesn't respond, doesn't acknowledge that I'm there at all.

My mother and Whasoon assure me that he knows it is me, but I don't believe them. I pat his hand, smile, and then stand up to shake more hands and greet more smiling faces. But it takes quite a while before I'm able to fully engage.

A few minutes later, my mother motions for us to sit on the floor. I sit next to Brad, and he gestures for Sam to sit with us so we can communicate with the others.

Suddenly, the two glass doors that lead into the kitchen slide open. Sungsoo and Sunbok emerge, carrying a round table loaded with food. It is four feet in diameter, and every inch is covered with some form of exotic fare. They return to the kitchen and bring in another table, and then another. We all sit on the floor around the three tables and feast. I feel unspeakable joy to see my family eating such wonderful foods.

A dozen little bowls filled with remarkable food are on the table closest to us. There is rice and several variations of kimchi: *paechoo* kimchi (cabbage), *yeolmoo* kimchi (radish top), and *altaleemoo* kimchi (radish). There is *tuhhuk* (hot pepper paste with root vegetables). There is fish, chicken, and egg, and several dishes I can't identify.

Chulsoo gestures for Brad to begin eating, but Brad has studied the Korean etiquette books. "I'll wait for Mother and Father to start," he says.

My mother giggles with delight that her American son-in-law knows Korean customs. She picks up her chopsticks and gets the feast started.

Everything is shared. Chopsticks fly as everyone reaches across the table to pick the food they want. It makes me think of fondue or raclette—dining that requires people to interact. It's perfect.

My mother offers to place food in my mouth with her chopsticks. I smile and accept a big piece of kimchi. This gives her great pleasure. It's so good to see her smile. I giggle as I try to imagine my American mother of Dutch and German descent feeding me potatoes or lasagna with a fork.

It's fun to share the Korean way, to express affection by placing food in each other's mouths. I start feeding Brad, and he does the same back. Everyone laughs.

Chulsoo says something to Sam.

"Kelly," Sam says, "Chulsoo wants to know if you are tired."

"Oh, thank you," I say. "I'm a little tired, but I'm enjoying myself very much."

"He wants you to know that he can bring you and the kids to your hotel anytime you want. Your family is enjoying having you here, but they want you to feel comfortable."

"Tell him I say, 'Thank you,' but I'm OK, and I want to stay."

Sam says something to my brother, and he smiles toward me and nods.

We stay several hours until the jet lag completely wipes us out.

It is past midnight when we get to the hotel. The bathroom has a tub and shower, and the room has a small refrigerator stocked with soft drinks and juices. There are two beds. Sam gives us a rundown of the next day's itinerary, but her speech is completely wasted. I'm too tired to absorb any of it.

Both Cici and Max have to be hauled into bed like sacks of potatoes. Brad jumps into bed and passes out immediately. A few minutes later I'm curled up next to him, wrapped in his warmth.

My Korean parents'
wedding.

My portrait, sent ahead
by the adoption agency.

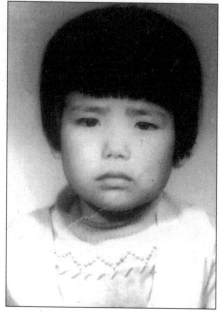

On Namsan Mountain, 1967. Namsan is in the heart of Seoul.

With Whasoon (left), 1970.

My grandfather.

Backrow: Myongsuk, Chulsoo, Whasoon, Pyongsoo, and Myonja. Frontrow: Father and Mother. My father's sixtieth birthday, a milestone birthday in Korea.

From left to right: Whasoon, Myongsuk, Myongja, Myonghi (me), Chulsoo, and Pyongsoo.

Being fitted for my wedding clothes at
my mother's friend's store in Geumsan.

With Whasoon, in 2008.

With my mother.

Brad, the children, and I with my brother, sisters, nieces, and nephews.

Myongsuk, Whasoon, me, and Myongja
on the beach on the Sea of Japan.

With Whasoon, my mother, Myongja, and Myongsuk.

Harvesting greens for making kimchi with
my mother in her front yard, Geumsan.

On Namsan Mountain, 2008.

Cici (right) and her cousin, Heywhan.

With Suzie, the first
day we met.

From left to right:
Max, Suzie, me,
and Cici, for Suzie's
first visit to our
home.

Fourteen

CATCHING UP

A<small>T SEVEN O'CLOCK THE NEXT MORNING, THERE'S A</small> knock on the hotel room door. I struggle out of bed and open it.

"Good morning," Sam says. "Did you sleep well?"

"The children were up several times, but otherwise it was a good night," I reply. I wish I could sleep an extra hour or so, but I don't say anything about how tired I am.

The children jump up and turn on Korean television cartoons. Brad lifts his head from his pillow and peers at us. "Hi, Sam," he says. "What's up for today?"

"We're going to Kelly's mother's house, and then we have to prepare. The family is taking you to a resort on the East Sea" (also known as the Sea of Japan).

An hour later, Chulsoo meets us in front of the hotel to take us to my mother's house.

Sunbok and Myongja greet me at the front door with bows and hugs. I walk into the bedroom where my mother is still getting dressed. She seems surprised to see me. I hug her. She giggles and gives me a smile and a pat on the back.

Father is fully dressed and laying on their bed. Myongja enters and starts sitting him up. Sunbok joins in, and they haul him to his feet. They walk him into the living room and set him on the chair next to the door again.

The kitchen doors open, and my family starts bringing in the food. They're treating us to another fantastic meal. My mouth waters in anticipation.

Once again, my mother sits next to me and takes my hand. "Being so skinny runs in our family," she says. "It's my fault you're so skinny."

"Sam," I reply, "tell her that it's OK. I like the way I am."

Sam tells her as my mother continues to hold my hand, patting my arm from time to time. Then she holds both of my hands together and looks directly into my eyes. She's been aching to tell me something.

"I kept telling everyone," she says, "that we would find you. I kept saying 'we will find her. We will find her.' Then I realized that I sent you away. I didn't have any right to expect you to come home. I'm so sorry." She starts to cry. "There wasn't a day I felt comfortable after sending you away. All I wanted was for you to forgive me."

"There are many opportunities that I never would have had," I say. Everything worked out. There is no reason for her to suffer anymore. Certainly, she shouldn't feel any shame. "Sam, tell her that it's OK. I'm fine."

Sam translates. My mother looks away, contemplating for a moment.

"Thank you," she says finally. Then she turns to Brad. "Thank you for taking such good care of my daughter."

Brad smiles and bows.

Brad catches my attention just as we finish stuffing ourselves.

"Is this a good time to pass out the gifts?" he asks.

"Oh, that's right!" I say as I get up and walk into the bedroom to retrieve the gifts.

I wheel a suitcase into the center of the living room. My mother sits next to my father, and everyone gathers around. I start first with my mother's gift, a large photo album filled with shots of me throughout the years. I want to give her a fill-in for all the years she missed. Just as I want the voids in my past filled, I want to fill them for her, too. But it suddenly feels so egocentric to present her with a photo album filled with pictures of me. It's too late to worry about that now. I give it to her using both hands, as I've been taught.

Her weathered hands loosen the tape gently. She is trying to open the gift without damaging the paper. It is her way of honoring the work I put into wrapping it. I hold my breath, hoping she will like it.

When she finally peels back the paper, a four-inch-by-six-inch picture of my smiling face jumps out at her. She realizes it is a photo album and lets out a joyful gasp. The rest of the family oohs and aahs. She looks up at me and smiles. My oldest sister Whasoon gives me an affirming grin to let me know that I have hit the mark. I smile in return, feeling a bit silly for worrying so much.

I sit on the floor in front of my mother, reach up, and open the book.

My father turns his eyes toward my picture. He keeps rocking back and forth, struggling to keep focus. There is still no sign that he recognizes me.

Sam interprets.

"This is my first American picture." I point to the 1971 picture of me from right after I got off the plane. "This is my mother, my brother, and my little sister." I let my mother and father study each photo for a moment or two before I move on. "This is my American grandfather. He's my mother's father."

I suddenly realize how opulent my parents' house must seem compared to the Korean house we used to live in. I hope they don't feel bad. It eases my guilt to see that my mother is living in such a nice house now.

Soon the whole family is straining to see the pictures of my late childhood and my adolescence. There are photographs of me with braces and seventies hair, of my American family camping and celebrating Christmases, of my summer in France and my travels throughout Europe. And, of course, there are plenty of pictures of Brad and the kids.

My mother smiles and squeezes my hand. Through Sam, she thanks me for the gift.

I stand up and pass out the other gifts. Each of my siblings gets a small photo album, an abbreviated version of my mother's. I also give each of the women lilac-fragranced hand soap. In accordance with what he was taught about Korean custom, Brad has packed little bottles of Jack Daniel's whisky for all of the men. I pass those out, too. Everyone receives their gifts graciously. They all seem pleased.

Chulsoo says a few words in Korean, and suddenly everyone starts getting up. A few minutes later, we all jump into the vans and cars. My family is taking us shopping. We need to get ready for the trip to a resort on the East Sea.

Brad and I are members of Costco, the giant warehouse club. I never dreamed when I became a member I'd be shopping at a Costco in Korea.

It turns out that Korea has six stores, including one in Daejon City. We go to the Daejon Costco because my family is worried that Cici and Max aren't eating enough. While everyone else has been feasting, my kids have been finicky. So my family is bringing us to a store that has some American-style foods.

I've never seen such a large store before—three floors packed with everything imaginable. No Costco in the United States is anywhere near this vast, as far as I know. All I want are a few little things, but everything of course is in huge packages.

My brother and sisters want to make sure I don't spend any money. Brad admires a box of assorted coffees, and one of my family members puts it in their cart. I look at the bulk packages of breakfast cereal, and then someone gets one and won't let me pay for it. I realize I have to be careful what I look at. My family is willing to buy as much as it takes to make me happy. I want to tell them it's not necessary. I'm just happy to be with them. But how does one say something like that without sounding ungrateful. I decide it's best to say nothing. Besides, I have to admit that it feels wonderful absorbing all the generosity, love, and attention they're showering upon me.

Our entire group of twenty browses when I browse and stops to look when I stop. Everywhere we go, we block the way of other shoppers, and I start to feel sorry about it.

We decide it's best if the group splits up. Chulsoo, Sunbok, and a bunch of others go off to stock up for the trip. Brad, Sam, Sungsoo, and I go in another direction.

Sungsoo is very sweet. Anytime we pay the slightest attention to a free sample, he gets some for all of us. Soon we've tasted pomegranate juice, vegetable juice, several brands of dip, and many types of crackers.

A man at the candy counter uses large shears to cut off pieces of hard toffee, one for each of us. It is light brown and hard as a rock. Through Sam, he warns us that we should not chew it or we'll be fishing goo out of our teeth for the next couple of hours. Hard toffee is meant to be sucked, he explains, not chewed.

"Do you remember this toffee from when you were growing up?" Sungsoo asks me via Sam.

"No, I don't."

"The toffee man would come around the neighborhood and snap his shears, making a loud sound. All the kids would come running. He'd trade pieces of toffee for pieces of scrap metal, things like old silverware. He also traded toffee for hair."

I look at Sam, then at Sungsoo. "Really?"

"Yes. Children would gather the hair that fell around the house and he'd collect it for the wigmaker."

"With five females living in the house," I say, "I bet my sisters and I traded a lot of hair for toffee."

I try to remember the sound of snapping shears echoing through the streets of Geumsan. But there's nothing. The taste is familiar, but it doesn't remind me of Korea. It reminds me of something I ate in Rochester, Minnesota, when I was little. A part of me feels sad that I don't recall eating this here. I want to remember so much more than I do.

I tell Sam that one of our family rituals in Minnesota is to buy pizza for the kids when we go to Costco. The next thing I know, the whole group is seated at a huge table, and pizzas are being passed around.

Unexpectedly, the store manager steps forward. There are a lot of smiles and lots of bowing, and suddenly the manager is treating all of us to dinner. Someone has told him my story, and he wants to make my family feel as welcome as he can.

Fifteen

SOKCHO

THE NEXT DAY WE DRIVE TO SOKCHO, A SMALL PORT city in the northern province of Gangwon-do, just south of the North Korean border. Fences topped with razor wire line many of the beaches there. There's still a worry that communist agents might sneak in. Or worse, that the North might send hit squads or launch a full-scale invasion.

We will be staying about twenty miles from the east end of the Demilitarized Zone (DMZ). The DMZ is a two-and-a-half-mile-wide no-man's-land that stretches 160 miles from the Yellow Sea to the Sea of Japan.

While I detest their tyrannical government, I think of the North Koreans as my people, in the same way I think of the South Koreans. I've been asked by some of my American friends why so many people followed Kim Il-Sung and now Kim Jong-Il. *Frightened people do what they can to survive* is my answer. If they fail to stand up against the craziness, it's because they fear for themselves and their families.

After terrorists slaughtered nearly three thousand people in New York City in 2001, my America was gripped by an understandable fear. My government proceeded to spend trillions of dollars and thousands of lives waging war against a country, Iraq, that was of little threat and had nothing to do with the attack in question. We even tortured people. As the old saying goes, hysterical sheep are more dangerous than wolves. Who am I to judge the North Korean people?

The four-hour drive to Sokcho gives my sisters and me time to talk. There are nine of us in the van, and Sam gets a workout translating all that we say to each other. Another van with other members of my family follows us. A few other family members will drive to the resort in their own cars later.

Whasoon, Myongja, and Myongsuk sit in the very back seat. Cici and I sit in the seats in front of them. Sam and Max take up the next row forward. Brad sits in the front passenger seat. Chulsoo is driving.

"I've been thinking," Whasoon says. "That memory of us doing wash by the river. I bet it was Chulsoo's diapers that we were washing."

Chulsoo blushes.

"Do you remember the orphanage?" Myongja asks me.

"I remember taking baths there and playing with the girl who would become my adopted sister."

Brad twists around in his seat. "Sam, could you ask what it was like for the family after Kelly left?"

She translates Myongja's answer, "Everyone was very sad after you left. It was very quiet."

"We were told," Whasoon adds, "that you would be put through an acclimation process, that you would especially need to get used to American food."

We all laugh.

"What about your father?" Brad asks. "Can you tell us more about him?"

"Father fought in the Korean Civil War," Whasoon says. "He was in the army—starting in his teens—for seven years. He was the eldest sibling in his family. He came from Hwasun, a small town near the southwest tip of the Korean peninsula. Before the war, his family was pretty well off, but after the war the family crashed. They became very poor. Mother's family was well off, but in Korean culture the woman marries into the man's family, and that determines her financial status."

As we drive northeast, the Korean countryside unfolds all around us: vistas of peaks and vales with differing hues of deep greens so thick that the earth is not visible save for the occasional rocky cliff. The misty white of low-lying clouds fills a valley from time to time, contrasting with the mountains and making the green look all the more vivid.

"In the United States we have an expression to describe this kind of scenery," Brad says. "We call it 'God's Country.'"

"Yes," Chulsoo says, nodding his head.

Brad turns to Whasoon. "In one of your e-mails to us, you wrote that Kelly loved to sing. Do you remember some of the songs?"

Whasoon nods enthusiastically, and almost immediately starts to sing. I can't believe how beautiful my sister's voice is. The melody is warm, touching, and haunting all at the same time.

I struggle to keep from crying, but it's no use. The melody and the sound of her voice touch my heart. I can't recall the Korean lyrics, but something deep inside me remembers the song. My chest swells, as I try to keep my emotions under control. I feel like a child again. I want to squeeze her hand even tighter and never let it go. I wipe the tears from my eyes, and soon Whasoon starts to cry, too. Myongja finishes the song for her.

"Sam, could you translate some of the song?" Brad asks.

She hesitates for a moment.

"Mother, Mother, where are you?" she says. "I'm waiting for you beneath the covers."

Suddenly Sam stops and the van goes silent.

After a moment, my sister Whasoon starts singing "Itsy Bitsy Spider" to break the heavy energy. And I join in. Then Brad and Cici do, too, complete with hand machinations. Then everyone joins in. Surprisingly, all my siblings know it. Chulsoo sings as he drives, a big smile on his face.

Chulsoo pulls the van into a driveway beneath a sign that reads THE 38TH MARINE RESORT. It's a brand-new building less than a hundred yards from the beach. Scuba tanks and wet suits are stacked neatly against a wall.

My family piles out of the two vans and files into the waiting area. The salty smell of the ocean wind envelops us.

Chulsoo talks to the manager for a moment, and then leads everyone up to the third floor. He opens the door to a huge, two-bedroom space with a vaulted ceiling and a large loft at the top of a steep, wooden staircase. There is a tall pile of quilts in a storage area at the top of the stairs, along with enough blankets and pillows for everyone. There is only one bed, however, and it's obviously reserved for my mother. A small refrigerator stands next to a couch. Otherwise, the room is completely void of furniture. There's only one bathroom, as well, even though nearly thirty people will share this one unit, from ages one to seventy-five.

There's no better way to get to know someone than to eat and sleep together, and it occurs to me that we'll be getting to know my family very intimately now. Brad's a very light sleeper and I have a troublesome disk in my lower back, so I realize we probably won't be getting too much sleep.

"Kelly," Sam says, "Chulsoo wants you to follow him."

Brad, Sam, Myongja, the kids, and I all march down the hallway after my brother. Chulsoo stops at one of the rooms along the way and inserts a keycard to unlock the door. It's a large, lovely room overlooking the beach with a queen-sized bed and hardwood floors.

"This is your room," Chulsoo says with a proud grin. "You and Brad will stay here. If you want the children to stay with you, that is fine. Otherwise, they are welcome to stay in the big room."

"This is so generous, Chulsoo," I say. "Thank you."

He nods enthusiastically and hands me the keycard.

They all file out and leave Brad and me alone. The two of us settle quickly into our room. I perch myself by the window and sit back to watch the waves roll in from across the Sea of Japan. Brad spreads out on the bed

In less than a half hour there's a knock on the door. It's Sam.

"Hello, Kelly," she says. "I'm sorry to bother you, but Max and Cici have gotten into a fight. Cici bit Max, and the family wants to know what to do."

By the time we arrive at the scene of the crime, everything is calm. My sisters have the food unpacked and spread out near a refrigerator. Some of the children are napping, while others are playing upstairs. Cici is sitting quietly, looking guilty and expecting trouble.

It turns out that one of my nephews had to pull my children apart. He explains to Brad what happened. Sam translates.

"Cici snatched two balloons that she thought belonged to her away from Max. A fight followed, and Cici eventually bit Max on the arm."

"I'm so sorry you had to deal with this," Brad says. "I'll take care of it."

Brad pulls Cici aside and starts speaking with her. But Cici is embarrassed and asks to receive her punishment out of the room, where the relatives can't see. Brad takes her to our room for a talk and a time-out.

I'm very embarrassed. Cici is nine years old. She hasn't bitten anyone in years, and suddenly she chooses to do it in front of my whole Korean family.

I decide to tell Myongja how embarrassed I am. I sit next to her on the lone piece of furniture, the loveseat. Whasoon sits down with us. Sam translates.

"I'm so sorry," I say.

"Kids are the same everywhere," Myongja says. "You know, you and I used to fight. We pulled each other's hair."

I remember her saying that on the bus ride from the airport. I have a faded memory of having a conflict with someone near my age. It's more of a feeling than a memory.

"I remember," Whasoon says, "that you couldn't stand my discipline. You used to say that I was bossing you around. You thought I was mean. You said that when you came back from America with an airplane full of money and food, that you wouldn't give any of it to me."

We laugh.

"Did mother and father fight sometimes?" I ask.

"Father was often very sick," Whasoon says. "He collapsed out in the field once and was in bed for a year. He rushed out during a storm to try to rescue the fields from flooding. They had to carry him back. One other time he was sick for four months."

"Father was a very kind person," Myongja adds. "He was generous with other people, considered like an angel. There is an old Korean saying, 'This person can live without laws.' That was your father. He didn't need rules to keep him on the straight and narrow. He didn't have any evil in him."

Chulsoo and my mother join us, and the next thing I know I'm surrounded by a crowd of my relatives again.

"Father was a war hero," Chulsoo tells me. "He was decorated for his actions in the civil war. All of the soldiers from his troop were wiped out except him and two other men. They hid in a cave, climbing out to find themselves behind enemy lines. Many soldiers in his day fled to the safety of Japan or to the safety of the Americans, but father chose to stay and to fight. Father fought in Gangwon-do, in the north. He was pushed back with many others, all the way to Busan. Then the American general MacArthur invaded and turned his fortune. Father fought back up into North Korea, but the Chinese pushed him back again. He was shot seven times."

"He loved his country and tried to protect it," Whasoon continued. "When he finished fighting in the war, he tried to become a farmer, but he wasn't very good at it. He wrote a diary during the war. Later, during hard times he attempted suicide. He burned many of his papers and medals. His diary was lost."

"Did any of his medals survive?" I ask.

"Yes," my mother says. "I have a vest that has many medals on it. I will show it to you when we return home."

Brad and Cici enter, and, like a switch has been thrown, all the kids jump up and head upstairs to play. My mother and my siblings stay with me.

"You know," my mother says, "you were your father's favorite."

I don't know how to respond. My sisters are sitting right there, and I don't want them to feel bad.

"Father really loved you," Whasoon adds.

"It must have been him," I respond. "I remember having such a strong connection to an old man. I thought it was Grandfather, but it must have been Father."

"Yes," Whasoon says, nodding her head with an affirming smile.

"I remember crawling across the floor and checking an old man's mouth for food in the middle of the night. He made a chomping sound in his sleep, and I checked in his mouth to see what he was eating. It had to have been him."

"Yes, it must have been Father," Myongja says.

"We didn't know we were giving you up," my mother says. "We knew you'd go away for a long time, but we thought you would be fed and educated and then come back to help with the family."

"You must be tired of talking," Chulsoo interjects suddenly. "Are you hungry?"

One minute later, I realize why he's asking, when a tray of fish is delivered to the room as if it were a pizza. The fish is cut and served to look like a flower. Chulsoo has ordered it from the fish stand just fifty feet from the resort's front door.

The tray is set on the floor in the center of the room, and we all gather around. I watch in amazement as everyone enthusiastically begins eating the raw seafood. My mother feeds Brad a few bites, which he graciously chews and swallows. I don't want to offend my family, but I just can't eat the raw fish. My stomach has not been normal since we arrived.

Later, we go to the resort bar. Someone brings in a birthday cake, complete with candles and sparklers. A huge grin spreads across Chulsoo's face as they slide the flaming confection in front of him and we all sing "Happy Birthday." I watch him glow with a joy brighter than the sparklers. I was in Korea when he celebrated his first birthday. I've missed all the others since. It feels good to be back for his thirty-eighth. It feels good to see him so happy.

Then everything breaks loose. Someone pulls out a microphone, and before I know it several of my relatives are up on stage, singing karaoke.

All at once my sisters Myongja and Myongsuk take over the stage and start singing. They keep gesturing in my direction, and I suspect they are singing a song dedicated to me. Sam leans over and tells me that the lyrics are, indeed, about loving me. A lump wells up in my throat.

After they are done singing, they turn the microphone toward me. They start clapping and cheering, and the whole bar joins in, trying to get me up on the stage.

"Only if Brad sings, too," I demand. I know Brad will refuse, and I'll be off the hook.

Everyone starts cheering Brad along, and they soon make it clear that they aren't going to stop unless we both get up and sing. Brad finally gets up on stage, and my bluff has been called. I have no choice; I have to join him. Brad asks if there is an acoustic guitar in the house. Someone passes one up, and everybody cheers some more.

"All right," Brad says, nervously fingering some chords to loosen up. "Now what the hell do we do?"

"'Ishq Allah'?" I suggest.

"I don't think they'd appreciate a Middle Eastern tune."

My family, and everyone else in the bar, starts to cheer and clap again. They're getting tired of our dithering.

"Let's do 'I'll Fly Away,'" I say.

"Okay," responds Brad, and we're off.

Some bright morning, when this life is over,
I'll fly away.

To that home on God's celestial shore,
I'll fly away,
I'll fly away, O Glory.
I'll fly away, in the morning.
When I die, Hallelujah by and by, I'll fly away.

We sound pretty anemic, and nobody other than Sam understands a word we're singing, but everyone in the entire bar has their hands up in the air, waving them back and forth to the gospel rhythm. They're all looking at my husband and me, which makes me feel like an insect in a glass jar. We make it through the song, and the entire bar erupts in applause and raucous cheers.

After several rounds of drinks, my nephew Sungsoo leads seven of us adults out of the building and along the beach frontage road, past a little seafood stand. We have no idea where we're headed. It turns out to be another karaoke bar.

Brad and I have never seen anything like it. It has six little rooms about the size of bedrooms. We enter one of the rooms and see a large television screen that takes up most of one wall. Benches line the perimeter, but most of the floor is left clear for dancing. A song I don't recognize is playing at a deafening volume. It reminds me a bit of a seventies discothèque. I'm afraid my ears will explode.

Everybody gets a turn at the microphone, even if they don't want one. Each of my siblings sings close up to my face, as a way of dedicating their particular song to me. Several dedicate songs to Brad in the same way. Those who aren't singing are dancing. I'm enjoying dancing with my sisters. Myongja is especially full of life. She has the animated personality and the man-nerisms of an actress. We jump around together, laughing and singing. It's so much fun.

When it's my turn, I choose "Dust in the Wind" by Kansas. I am relieved to find that the microphone provides enough reverb to make me sound pretty good, and I am surprised to discover that all my relatives know the words.

Back at the resort, with our ears still ringing, we gather on the floor to talk some more. A few of the older children are still awake, glued to the television. The younger kids are sleeping, so we adults are left to talk in relative quiet.

My mother, sisters, and I compare the features of our hands and feet. We're amazed at the similarities. One of my sisters shows me that my fourth toe on each foot is bowed inward, toward the big toe. We all have that same strange little bow. Myongja's hands and feet look almost exactly like mine. Myong-suk and I share the same neck and ears. I thought I'd never be able to compare my genetic features with anyone. It feels fantastic.

I look closely at my mother's face, trying to see myself, and for a fleeting instant I can discern that her nose and lips are something like mine.

Whasoon notices me studying my mother's face. "You know," she says, "when Father was sick, Mother had to take over and do all of the work. She was in the fields from morning until night. That is probably why you don't remember her. She was too busy trying to feed the family. She went without food many times so we could eat."

I study my mother's face again. I wonder if she knows how

much I admire her for what she managed to do, how she survived while carrying the weight of the whole family. I doubt I would have been so strong. I'm proud to be her daughter.

"Was it that way for a long time?" I ask.

"Not long after you left, things got better and we were able to build a new house," Whasoon says. "Father was unable to get out of bed almost a year before that, but then he improved."

If I had stayed just a little bit longer, I would still be part of this family. I would know my father, and he would know me. They wouldn't have to tell me the family stories. I would know the narrative because I would have been a part of it. I would be speaking Korean. I would be married to a different man, and I wouldn't have Cici and Max.

Sixteen

THE OCEAN'S A BIG ERASER

T HE NEXT DAY, WE TRAVEL TO A SPA SOMEWHERE IN THE
hills north of Sokcho: Six adults and nine children in two
vans. Chulsoo pays for all of us to get in.

The place is huge, half the size of the Mall of America, with
over a thousand people in the many indoor and outdoor pools
or the food court. Only about five out of the whole crowd are
Caucasian, and I'm married to one of them.

Brad seems to enjoy the attention he's getting, especially
from Korean children. Many of them point or simply walk up
and stand in front of him, slack-jawed. When a group of school-
girls passes by, one of the girls giggles and shouts, "Hello!" Brad
laughs and shouts back, "Yo, Adrian," mimicking Sylvester Stal-
lone's character Rocky Balboa in *Rocky*. The pool area echoes
with a gaggle of little Korean girls laughing at my husband.

We pass by the hydraulic wave pool. Immediately outside the terrace door is a basin with hot-spring water flowing
through it. We use wooden bowls to pour the water over our
bodies. It feels wonderful as it contrasts with the cool mist
coming down. We descend several flights of stairs to a series of

soaking pools, which have been built into the landscape, complete with stone gardens, plants, and trees. Brad and I soon find ourselves with Chulsoo, Sungsoo, and Whasoon soaking in the purplish color of a lavender pool. We sit until our skin puckers, then immerse ourselves in a pool with jets of hot water. Next we move on to the massage pool, which has individual stations where water shoots out at my legs and back. I've died and gone to heaven.

We move on again, and I decide against the pool with the fish that nibble off your dead skin. Since I'm the guest of honor, everyone else skips that one, too. Instead, our group heads for the canal pool in which people with inner tubes float around lazily. The canal water is cold, so after only a moment or two of floating and freezing, we hop out and scurry to the largest indoor pool: the pool of magical water devices, with dozens of different kinds of whirlpools, gushers, and powerful jets. My favorite is a giant chrome showerhead about six feet tall. It shoots a powerful stream of water onto the neck and upper back.

About twenty percent of South Koreans are Buddhists, and I wonder if any of them realize that nirvana is right here, in this spa.

When we return to the resort, some members of my family are working on a barbeque feast. Three picnic tables are overflowing with food, with two large grills manned by Myongja's husband and Sungsoo. As soon as we drive up, we're ushered into the banquet.

As I scan the maze of salads and cut fruit, I can't help but marvel at how different things are now from when I was a child, when we counted ourselves lucky if we had one meal a day. I see platters overflowing with melons, bowls filled with rice, all kinds of beer, flavored waters, and juices.

As I walk past one of the grills, Myongja's husband grabs a pair of chopsticks, picks out a piece of meat, wraps it in lettuce, and puts it in my mouth. It tastes fantastic, so delicately salted with just the right mix of spice and herbs, and the moist lettuce punctuates the symphony of tastes with a crisp freshness.

I chew and nod. "Thank you."

He smiles and bows, turns in the other direction toward Brad and does the same. Brad looks confused at first, not knowing if it's a joke, then smiles and bows back. (When he bows, my husband looks like a stork bobbing for crabs. Koreans tend to bow from the neck. My husband is tall and bows in the Japanese manner, from the waist.)

Then, Sunbok wraps some lettuce around a piece of pork and puts it in my mouth. Then I remember that in Korea, feeding each other is an informal way of showing respect and love. I look over and see Brad feeding meat back to my brother-in-law.

I join in. I feed a piece of meat wrapped in lettuce to Whasoon. Suddenly, I realize that I've made a mistake. I should have fed a piece to my mother first. I take the best-looking piece of meat I can find, wrap it in a lettuce leaf, and walk over to my mother. She smiles approvingly and opens her mouth. I put it in and pat her on the arm. Then I go around and feed my two other sisters.

Brad is sitting across from Sungsoo and one of my other nephews. They're drinking beer together. As Korean etiquette requires, each young man shields his face with his free hand and turns away from Brad with every sip. Brad looks confused. He starts to tease them by pretending to hide under the table each time he raises his glass. The three of them share a good laugh. The contrast is striking: the informal, older American, and the two, very formal young Koreans.

The next morning, Brad tries to sleep in, but Max is up and moving around early. I'm awake, too. I want Brad to get as much sleep as he can, so I decide to take Max out of the room and down to the beach. It will be fun to see the first time Max has ever touched ocean water, and he will be doing so on my native earth. Sixty years from now, he'll be telling his grandchildren my story.

The two of us walk out of the front of the resort and stroll up and down along the surf, searching for shells and skipping stones. Eventually, Max writes his name in the wet sand, then watches as the surf rolls over it.

"Mom, the ocean's a big eraser, isn't it?" Max says.

"What do you mean, Max?"

"Well, when you write your name in the sand and the wind makes the waves go up, they erase everything."

I look out at the Sea of Japan and the Pacific Ocean beyond. When I crossed it in 1971, leaving everything behind, my whole world was effectively erased. I was given a new name, a new mother and father, new brother and sisters, a new culture, and a new language. Thousands of miles of waves erased who I was.

Now, magically, the person I once was has reappeared, on the same side of the ocean as where I was born.

"Yes, Max. You're exactly right. The ocean is a big eraser."

"I don't want the next few days to pass," my mother sighs. "I'm afraid I'll never see you again in this life."

We're sitting on her living room floor in Geumsan. It's late in the evening, and we've been back from the resort for several days. Chulsoo and his wife, Sunbok, are with us, too. Sam is translating.

My whole body aches with sadness at the thought of leaving. It's going to be much more difficult than I expected. My Korean family is firmly placed back in my heart and soul now. I wish I could make the trip last longer.

"I have something to say to you both," Chulsoo says. "It is important, and I have been waiting for the right moment."

I study his face. He is so beautiful. He is polite and courteous to his wife. He's gentle and loving to his children. He is the individual I will speak of when asked by Americans about Korean men.

My mother stands, as if cued, and goes into her bedroom.

"I have things to tell you, and they are very difficult," Chulsoo continues. "There have been many things going on, and I needed to wait until things calmed down."

What could be said that I haven't already heard? Why would he have to wait to tell me something? Brad and I exchange glances.

Chulsoo hesitates, preparing in his mind what he will say. He glances down for a moment, clears his throat, and then turns his eyes back up toward mine.

"Father didn't just support our family," he says. "He was supporting fifteen people, including members of the extended family. There was a time when, if we had one meal in a day, we were doing well. Father was the oldest brother in his family, and it fell on him to take care of the family. But he was overwhelmed with the responsibility.

"Some family members took advantage of his kindness. Our father's father tried to start a business, but he failed and went into debt. Father inherited grandfather's debt. Father was a responsible man and an honest man, so he had to pay off the creditors while supporting the whole family.

"He became physically and mentally worn out. He was in bed for a year. We didn't think he'd ever get up. Mother was left with the whole burden. Many of those around her suggested sending a child or two away for adoption. They warned her that that was what she should do if she wanted her children to live. That's when you, Myonghi, were given up for adoption.

"Mother said she would never give up one of her children. But a local official lied to her. He said there was an educational opportunity. He presented it as a sponsorship rather than an adoption. Mother and Father were told that you would go away for a long time, but you would be sent back home after college. She wouldn't have to wait thirty-seven-years to see you again. She was told that you would send letters and be able to correspond. No one else would be called *Mother* or *Father*. Mother didn't understand that it was an adoption. Father and Mother were lied to by the official. But mother took all of the blame.

"A little while after you went to the States, a letter came. No one could read the letter because it was in English. Mother believed that it was the first of many letters and that they would keep coming. There was a picture of you in the envelope. Mother stuck the picture to the wall.

"When she realized that she had been lied to, she tried to rip the picture off the wall. But she had used glue. There was writing on the back, and she thought it might be an address or some other information. The writing had stuck to the wall, and there was no way to read it. Back then there was no one here who could speak anything other than Korean. The letter got handed from one relative to another, and eventually it was lost."

I am stunned: my adoption was a forced adoption. When I think of how loving my family is and how much they suffered because I was gone, the news makes perfect sense. As I listen to Chulsoo, I try to imagine what it must have been like for my mother—the horror of finding out that your child had been given away without your consent. It must have been terrible.

"For years Mother would cry, *Myonghi! Myonghi!*" Chulsoo continues. "She always cried your name, and she always blamed herself. But she never wanted to give you up.

"Even after so many years we are family, and you are always my sister," Chulsoo adds. He turns to Brad. "And you are always my brother."

Chulsoo looks back at me. He hesitates, but it is clear that he has more to say. I keep silent and let him continue.

"About Father. . . . He was a very kind man, a man of few words. He slept only three hours a day and worked the rest. Even after he didn't have to work, he kept working. He couldn't stop. Some relatives used him and pressured him to give them money. Because of what happened it is hard to be around some relatives. Some of them took advantage of him."

Sunbok cuts in: "Your father only scolded me once. We were walking down the street, and I took a cherry from a branch that was hanging over someone's fence. He scolded me for taking that cherry. He was the most honest man I've ever met."

"Because Father was sick," Chulsoo says, "Mother would leave early for work and come home late. When she came home she always had chores to do. A lot of the responsibility for the family fell on Mother.

"I wanted to tell you these things so you would know the truth," Chulsoo continues. "Father and Mother didn't abandon you. They didn't want to give you up. They only wanted for you to eat and to be educated."

Chulsoo has taken his place as the eldest male of the family. I'm so proud of him. I look at him and see the obvious love and respect he has for our mother and father. A strange feeling of relief comes over me because of what he's told me. Someone had to trick my parents in order to take me from them!

As I lie in my hotel bed that night, I struggle to make sense of the new information I've been told. My family never wanted to give me up. They were lied to. I was loved, not abandoned or rejected like I'd always feared. And it wasn't my grandfather who'd been so kind to me. That was a memory I created, a construct. My father was almost forty in 1971. Of course, a little girl would think of a sickly forty-year-old as a grandfather. It had been my father who was so ill. It was his mouth I checked for food in the middle of the night when the hunger made my body ache. It was he who loved me so dearly. I am sure of that now.

In the morning, after breakfast, Whasoon offers to take me on a walk to see some of the places where I spent time as a child. I agree, hoping that some of the old sights will stir up more memories. Brad and Sam come with us.

First, we walk to where my old home used to be. It stood only a hundred yards or so away from where my mother's house is today. When the main road came through, the old house must have been in the way. There's just a big, black span of tar there now. Whasoon has to take me out to the middle of the road before we can stand on the exact spot. She moves around, pointing and gesturing, as if she's mapping out the floor plan on the asphalt.

"The door was here," she points. "And we slept over there. The kitchen was over there, and here is where the entrance was."

"I remember that the kitchen was separate and the floors were heated by fire," I say. "The house had a tin roof. I remember hearing the rain against the tin. And a brick wall went around the yard, with large gates at the entrance."

She smiles and nods. It's exciting to be standing on the exact location of my childhood home. As far as I'm concerned it's hallowed ground. I think back to Whasoon cooking, her skirt touching the floor, and that old clay oven with the wood burning in it.

Whasoon points toward a mountain less than a mile away.

"Do you recognize that?" she asks.

"I'm afraid I don't."

"That was what you looked at every day as a child. It hasn't changed."

I gaze at the mountain. It's beautiful. I see a place cleared from the hillside with what looks to be monuments or gravestones, and a small pagoda with what appears to be an area for people to sit. I ask Sam to explain.

"Those are graves," she says. "The stone tablets are tables for the tomb. In Korea, during national holidays such as the *chooseok*—our thanksgiving—or during the lunar New Year celebrations, all families hold a memorial service. And the stone tablets are used as tables to place the food and wine we offer to our ancestors."

I remember when I vacationed with my American family in Vancouver, British Columbia. I looked up at the Canadian Rockies and said to my American mother, "The mountains are so beautiful. I really miss them." She corrected me, saying that I had never been to the mountains before. She was the adult, so I figured that she was right. But I was confused. Somewhere in my bones I felt that mountains were something sacred and precious to me.

Suddenly, we have to run toward the curb because a truck is barreling toward us. The truck passes, and we move onto the sidewalk. Whasoon guides us toward a row of houses, each surrounded by its own brick wall.

"Are there any other places around here that haven't changed since Kelly was young?" Brad asks.

Whasoon nods and leads us to where the walls of the adjoining houses form a narrow alley. We pass through and come to a small ginseng garden that is covered by black mesh attached to wood slats stuck in the earth. Whasoon is talking a mile a minute. I can't understand a word of it, and Sam is lagging behind. So I gesture, indicating that we should wait for Sam to catch up. She does.

"This alley was here when you were young," Whasoon says. She pulls me further down the alley and points to a field. "Our family rented that field."

"I remember it being much larger and more open."

"It *was* more open," Whasoon says. "Much of the land around has been built over now."

She pulls me along to a small canal with a trickle of water flowing through it. "This is the stream where we washed clothes," she says.

I can't believe my eyes. The entire stream has been lined with concrete, and the current has been reduced to a dribble barely two feet wide. My heart sinks. This stream had been one of my fondest memories of Korea. I remember the sun dancing across the water like white butterflies, and Whasoon's young hands working the wet clothes against the rocks. I feel like crying.

"They changed it a lot," Whasoon adds.

That is the understatement of the century.

"What about the hay shed?" I ask. "I remember lying in a hay shed and looking out the roof boards up to the sky."

"That was torn down and rebuilt every year," Whasoon explains. "The one you remember was probably torn down not long after you laid in it. When it got too hot in the summer, we would sleep in the sheds at night."

My memory had shrunk the hay shed to something about four feet by four feet. It must have been bigger for my whole family to have slept in it. As an American child, I often tried to recapture the feeling I took from that shed. I would draw clouds and sheds with pencils and crayons. I used to lie on my back in the grass and gaze at the clouds rolling over the eastern edge of Minnesota's prairie lands.

We walk down the alley back past Mother's house, to a little road paved with gravel.

"This has not changed," Whasoon says. "It is the same as when you were here. There was a store there." She points to a house on the corner. "Do you remember it?"

"I remember a little store. It was dirty and dingy. It had a post sticking out of the ground. It must have been in front of that store where I was bitten by the dog. Do you remember that?"

The dog had been tied to the post, and I tried to estimate the length of its leash. I misjudged, and the dog attacked me. I pull up my dress to show the scar on my calf.

"I wasn't there when the dog bit you, but I remember putting medicine on the wound."

As we walk from the shade of the houses out into the open, the hot sun beats down on my head. I made the mistake of wearing a black synthetic dress. All I can think of now is getting back into Mother's house to sit in front of her air conditioner. I start to feel shaky from the heat.

Whasoon seems to be reading my mind. She takes my hand and helps me along.

Not a square foot of black soil is wasted in Geumsan. Every little space that isn't concrete has some kind of food growing in it. My mother's front yard is covered with vegetables. So are many of the banks of the ditches and boulevards.

Whasoon points to an apartment building on the other side of a field. "That's where the playground used to be," she says. "You played there all the time."

I don't remember it. I try to imagine myself playing there, but nothing emerges.

It feels good when we get back into the cool air of Mother's living room. The clock on the wall indicates that it's nearly noon. It is blistering hot outside, and the humidity makes the air thick and hard to breathe.

I take the opportunity to reminisce with my mother.

"Tell me more about Father when I was little," I say to her.

"You used to get upset when Father would lift heavy things in the hay shed," she says. "You used to cry and plead with him to stop."

"Why?" I ask.

"You said you were afraid something might fall on him and kill him. It was very smart of a toddler to think of such things."

"Whasoon said something about me playing at the playground near our field," I say. "What do you remember about that?"

She hesitates, looks down at the floor and fiddles with her fingers, as if she is twisting some invisible string.

"You used to play on the playground," she says finally. "You played there often while I worked in the field. You loved to swing on the swing. One day you were swinging and fell off. You hit the back of your head on the ground. I heard you calling for me over and over again, but I thought you were just trying to fool me. When you didn't stop calling for me, I realized that you were really hurt. When I picked you up, you asked me why I didn't come."

I take her hands and squeeze them gently between mine. Forty years after making a very understandable mistake—one any parent might make—and my mother still feels guilty.

"You used to talk about going to America to get rich and buy me a house," Mother says, repeating the story I've heard several times now. "You were going make a lot of money to bring back to Korea."

I can't believe I came up with that idea without someone planting it in my head. Not at five years old. Someone must have been preparing me to go.

"You were excited to go for a ride in the car," Mother says. "But when you got in and realized I was not coming, you tried to get out. You cried and screamed for me. It was awful to see my daughter crying and calling out for me." My mother's voice starts to quiver. She struggles to keep her composure. "I cried for weeks."

Suddenly, the memory comes back to me in full: the woman with the shiny legs. I got into the big car with her. I thought it was a ride. The car was so beautiful, so opulent. I was fascinated by the seats, the doors, the windows. My mother was supposed to get in, but she didn't. I was excited at first, and then I panicked. It was horrible. I was terrified and confused as we drove away. I didn't understand what was going on that day, but my mother did. It was worse for her than for me.

"Don't feel bad," I say. "You did what was necessary at the time. I don't feel any anger about it."

I know how my mother feels. The day I gave up my daughter, Suzanne, a part of me was torn away. I don't think I'll ever get it back. The heartache didn't ease until my second child, Cici, was born.

Chulsoo and Sungsoo enter the room and sit down. The conversation turns.

"Your father liked to take you and Myongja on his bicycle," Mother says. "One day Myongja was on the back and you were on the handlebars. He accidentally hit the curb and tipped the bike over. In those days, the sewer water ran down the gutter of the street. He spilled you into the gutter, and the two of you were covered with filth. You both started yelling." My mother begins to laugh. "You were in front of the house. I could hear you yelling as you ran up. Mama! Mama! Daddy dropped us in the mess!"

It is good to see my mother laugh. She, like me, will always have that profound wound. She missed out on the life of her daughter. Neither of us will ever be able to turn the clock back. The wound inflicted by the loss of a child never completely heals.

Such a strange place for us to come together. Such a sad state of solidarity.

Seventeen

GIFTS

C HULSOO, MY SISTERS, AND MY MOTHER LEAD US TO A store in Geumsan's market district. It is owned by Mother's friends, and is in a row of buildings that reminds me of a Midwestern farmer's market. Each store is not much bigger than a shopping mall kiosk. My mother's friend's store is essentially a room on a platform two feet above the street. Folded garments and yards of fabric cover three of the walls, from floor to ceiling. A small fan fastened to a beam near the door is doing a poor job of cooling the steamy summer air.

We leave our shoes in the street and climb up. The woman gets everyone something refreshing to drink as her husband digs through a pile of clothes, looking for something suitable for my kids. Brad and I sit on the floor; my mother and siblings are across from us. Sam sits next to me, ready to translate.

"I remember you when you were a little girl," my mother's friend says. "Your mother cried so much when you went away. She ruined all of our gatherings after that, you know. Every time we started to have fun, she would burst out crying. She would always cry your name."

My mother looks embarrassed.

Suddenly, the store owners and Whasoon surround Cici, all talking at once. They decide to try several different outfits on her. The first is a blousy, yellow lace skirt with a yellow silk top. I can tell by her face that Cici isn't thrilled. She scrutinizes a few folded dresses and finally points to a pink one.

"I'd like to try this one on," she says. "It has yellow on the top, but it has lots of pink, too."

They put it on her, and she pirouettes like a Korean fairy-tale princess.

Then the group turns to working on Max. He tries on several outfits and finally decides on violet-colored silk pants and a blue coat with blue-, violet-, and white-striped sleeves. The kids look like Asian royalty.

"They are going to buy you a dress, too," my mother's friend says as she pulls me to my feet. "It is tradition for your family to buy your wedding clothes. Your mother says that she was not there when you were married, so they are going to buy them for you now."

"Oh, no," I say. "I couldn't."

Sam looks at me from across the room with her cute, eighteen-year-old Korean deadpan. "This is Korea, Kelly," she growls. "These are your relatives, and they want to give you something. If you don't take it, you will insult them."

I hesitate for a moment. My family looks at me.

"Okay," I say with a smile and a bow. "Thank you so much." My mother's friend immediately starts stretching a measuring tape over my shoulders, around my waist, and along my arms. She mumbles a few words to her husband, and he starts digging through the stacks of dresses.

He finally pulls out a red silk dress, as well as a pink coat with embroidered flowers on the shoulders. I put it on as my mother watches. It makes her very happy.

While I am adjusting the dress, my mother's friend slips a pink headpiece onto my head. It has red, yellow, and blue tassels and pearls strung across one side. Now *I* look like a Korean princess.

"This type of dress," Sam says, "is called a *hanbok*. It is a traditional Korean dress."

"It's beautiful, Mom," says Cici. She comes over and gives me a big hug.

When they're done with me, they start on Brad. He can barely stretch the first coat over his shoulders. It's made of silk and very handsome, but he looks like a bumpkin whose clothes have been washed in hot water and shrunk. The room erupts in laughter at the sight of him. Brad tries on a second coat that doesn't fit him much better. Finally, someone runs down the street to another store and comes back with a red-and-blue cotton top with matching red pants.

"Your suit, Brad," Sam says, "is a *gaeryang hanbok*. It's a modern-style version of the traditional Korean outfit for men."

Later, we walk down a busy street and my sisters buy more gifts for me. First, they provide me with two carved wooden masks that have been carefully packed with tissue inside a box. One is the face of a man, the other the face of a woman. I'm informed that the woman represents a bride, and the man a groom. My sisters are giving me one more belated wedding gift. I'm deeply touched. I bow and thank them from the bottom of my heart.

Then they give me a beautiful, inlaid jewelry box and take

me to a ginseng store, where I'm allowed to buy candies, tea, and liquor.

I feel satisfied knowing that my loved ones' days are no longer filled with hunger. Just like me, they have nice homes. They can feed their children, and they eat well, too. They have time and money to enjoy the good things in life. God bless South Korea.

"I have to leave for my job now," Myongsuk says. "It has been so nice to shop with you."

"Shop *for* me," I say, as I hug her. "Thank you so much."

"And I have to go to," Myongja says. "My children will be home too long without my husband."

I hug her, too. They both disappear down the street, and the rest of us go off to a restaurant for dinner.

My family decides to take me to the nursing home to visit my father. To my surprise, I am frightened by the prospect. I don't fear seeing my father; I fear seeing the nursing home. I'm afraid that the place will be rundown or dirty, and that it might make me even sadder about his condition than I am already.

On the other hand, I'm relieved that I'm going to see him once more before we leave. Now I'm sure that he is the old man I remember, and I want to speak to him at least once more.

The nursing home is a ten-minute drive from my mother's house in Geumsan. It's a professional-looking, brick building squeezed between a hospital and a small parking lot. We enter through a sliding glass door and are required to take off our shoes and put on slippers.

My fear about the facility melts away as soon as I see the bright, clean floors and well-maintained rooms. Several of the employees smile as we walk through, which reassures me that Father is being treated well.

Whasoon goes ahead of the rest of us to make sure that all my father's roommates are dressed before we enter their room. When we get there, she is standing in the doorway, smiling and motioning us to enter.

My father's room has seven beds, with each occupant suffering from some degree of dementia. One fellow with Down syndrome is on a mattress on the floor, presumably because he is in danger of falling out of a regular bed.

My sisters help my father to sit up with his legs crossed in the lotus position. My sisters massage his shoulders, then hug and kiss him and massage his hands.

Father's silver hair has been cropped close to his head. His pajamas are in immaculate condition. It's obvious that he's been recently bathed. Someone has shaved him, too, but they missed several long facial hairs growing out of his cheek.

As he did at my mother's house, Father rocks slowly back and forth. As before, his gaze drifts from time to time to meet my eyes, then falls back down again. At times, he simply stares downward, as if he doesn't want to deal with all the commotion.

My sisters begin to cry as they try to get him to recognize me. "Father, it's Myonghi. She's here to see you."

Faded blue rings have begun to form around his irises, making me wonder how much he can see.

"Father, it's Myonghi. She's here to see you," they say again. "Your daughter, Myonghi, from America has come to visit you."

My sisters ask me to sit at the foot of his bed. I do, and take his hand in mine. It is frail and cool to the touch. His skin is smooth and leathery. My sisters keep repeating, "Myonghi's here, Myonghi's here," gesturing toward me and crying as they rub his shoulders.

Suddenly, he tries to speak. Whasoon and Myongja both indicate that they can't understand him.

Whasoon takes his teeth from a cup on the nightstand next to his bed. She and Myongja fumble them into his mouth. He mumbles something into Myongja's ear, but she still can't make out what he's saying.

Chulsoo steps up to the bed. My father mumbles a single word, and my sisters cheer.

"He recognizes Chulsoo. He is saying Chulsoo's name."

Chulsoo puts his ear to my father's mouth, and my father mumbles something more. Chulsoo's signature grin spreads across his face instantly.

"He's asking about your children. Where are your children?" Chulsoo says. "He knows it's you. He remembers your children."

My siblings share a giddy surge of joy.

"They're at Mother's house," Chulsoo says to my father.

My father struggles to say more, and Chulsoo strains to understand him. I can see my father starting to cry. Myongja and Whasoon begin mopping the tears from his cheeks.

"He's saying he's sorry," Chulsoo says. "He's sorry for giving you up and what you had to go through."

"You have nothing to be sorry about," I say to my father, as I, too, begin to weep.

"He says that he loves you," Chulsoo continues. "And he's saying that he hopes you have a long life."

"I love you, too," I say to my father.

I am crying so hard now that I have to take a moment to catch my breath. "You did the best that you could. Times were hard and you did the best that you could."

"Myonghi ya," my father says. "Myonghi ya." It's what my mother called me the first time she saw me.

"You don't have anything to be sorry about." I desperately want him not to feel bad.

I lean forward and hug him. He is so tiny. I hold him in my arms. Everyone around me is watching and crying, too.

Twenty minutes go by before I find the strength to tear myself away from him.

"You take care of yourself," I say. "The love you showed me is still with me. I'll try as hard as I can to come back to Korea and see you again."

Even as I say this, I know that I will probably never see my father again. He's too frail. The dementia that is ravaging his mind has taken almost all of him away.

Outside my father's room a minute later, I fall apart. Brad holds me as I sob.

Since meeting my Korean father again, I have realized that my capacity to love is greater than I'd thought. When I lived in Korea—even though I was starving and sometimes could only dream about food—his love fed me. His love made the pangs of starvation less painful. I barely remember this old man, yet I love him so dearly. Seeing his face opened my heart again and reconnected me to the love I've carried since I was a little girl. It meant so much to me that in the end he really did know who I was. And now I remember him.

When I think back to some of the pejorative things I've heard about Korean men, I wonder what men they're talking about. My brothers are kind and loving to their families. My nephew is the model of decency. My father's kindness is and always has been the light that has led me through difficult times.

I know now deep in my heart that I was loved since birth. I am in contact again with the energetic, optimistic, outgoing little Korean girl. I have reclaimed her.

I am about to leave South Korea and return to Minnesota. Whasoon, Mother, and I sit on the floor in Mother's living room. Everyone has agreed to leave us alone for a while. Sam is in the room to translate, but she sits away, giving us the space to grieve.

I wrap my arms around Whasoon and hold on. My mother rubs my shoulder, trying to ease the pain of saying good-bye.

"I didn't think it would be this hard," I say.

My mother pulls me away from Whasoon and holds me.

Whasoon strokes my hair and then rubs my back. She pushes the hair back from my face and wipes the tears that are streaming down my cheeks.

My mother cradles my face in her hands. I can see her chin quiver as she tries to speak. "It is painful to let you go again," she says. "This is the second time I have lost my daughter."

"I'll be back, Mother. I'll come back as soon as I can."

"I'm afraid you will never see Father again in this world," she says. She takes off her glasses and wipes the tears away. "And I'm afraid I might never see you again, either."

"I'll come back. I promise."

My three sisters, my mother, Chulsoo, and Sungsoo drive us to the airport. We are silent most of the way. Whasoon holds my hand. She sings to me in her sweet voice, the Korean lullaby again:

Mother, Mother, where have you gone?
Where have you gone, leaving me under the covers?
Baby, don't cry. Don't cry.
Here, wear my dress.
No, no, Mother, I don't want to.
I want to fall asleep in your loving arms.

⚬

At the Incheon airport, my family treats us to one last Korean meal at a fancy restaurant above the main terminal. Other than some small talk about the food, we say very little. Mostly we sit quietly, looking sad and bewildered.

"I'm afraid we have to get going," Brad says, finally. Brad and I express our gratitude for everything my family has given us, and we begin to make our way to the security checkpoint. My family won't be able to accompany me past this point.

My mother starts crying first. Because of her bad back, she's been given a wheelchair. She looks so sad. The crying spreads from her to my sisters, until it takes over everyone. Cici is sobbing, and Max is, too. Brad struggles to keep his composure, and eventually fails. The people walking by stare at us.

"I am going to miss you so much," my mother says, holding my hands against her face. "Myonghi-ya! My Myonghi-ya, I am going to miss you so much."

"I'm so glad that I made this trip," I say, looking through my tears into my mother's eyes. "I will see you again. I will come back."

Whasoon steps forward and says some things to me in Korean. Sam can't translate because she is crying, too.

My sisters and I all take turns hugging one another. I hug Sungsoo and Chulsoo.

"I don't want to go home," Cici complains. "I want to live here."

I've not seen my daughter cry this hard before. Max walks around hugging his new relatives and crying.

We turn and walk slowly toward the sliding doors. My family is behind us.

"Myonghi-ya!" my mother cries out. "Myonghi-ya!"

Brad and I are weeping so hard that, after we pass through the doors, we turn the wrong way.

We stop and turn back to look at my family one last time. I wave good-bye. They wave back, and I hear my mother call my Korean name one last time, "Myonghi-ya!" The doors slide shut, and I am gone from them again.

I am barely conscious passing through security. Like a robot, I put my bags on the conveyor belt for the X-ray machine. Brad and Max are sniffling; Cici is weeping outright.

Once again, I'm on a plane, flying away from my Korean family, across the Pacific Ocean to America. Once again, I'm leaving them behind. I think of the warmth and love they've showered on me.

"I want to go back," Cici says.

"I want to live in Korea," Max adds.

I know how they feel. A part of me wants to go back and live there, too. But that's not where I belong. I am an American. I am married to an American man, and my children are American. It's time for me to go home.

When we arrive home, there is an email from Sam. She writes that my mother melted down at the airport after I left. She was so overcome with grief that she was unable to pull herself together. The others nearly called an ambulance to take her to the hospital.

Two days later, I receive this e-mail from my mother:

Kelly (Myonghi),
I was in break-hearted when I had no choice but letting little-you go to the state. I was glad to see you. And I appreciate that

you have been grown up so well. I am not sure when we see each other, however, I hope you to have a good time until that. Plus, I will see your picture, again and again. And I love your reliable and kind husband, Brad.

I thank you again about that you understand us.

My daughter. . . . I love you so much and miss you.

Your Mother

Eighteen

DEPARTURES

I ALWAYS LOVED THE TIME I SPENT WITH MY AMERICAN cousins, aunts, uncles, and grandparents. As I grow older, these connections fade. I hardly see them. The United States is so big, and my American family is widely dispersed. We're only three children now, and my parents. My parents live about a ninety-minute drive south of me, and my brother is about two hours away. My sister lives in Washington, D.C., several days' drive away. My parents travel overseas quite often, and spend lots of time in the southern parts of the United States.

My Korean family hasn't taken the place of my American one. No one could. But reuniting with the Korean family was, for lack of a better word, *mystical*, and it has reignited a feeling of completeness in me.

I love my Korean family, and it's my most profound wish to keep our new connection alive.

It has been months since we returned, and I'm finally gaining the emotional strength to contact my daughter, Suzanne. I feel the same fear that stopped me from contacting my Korean family for so many years.

Suzanne's parents sent pictures and letters for years after I gave her up for adoption. But all correspondence came to an abrupt halt at some point. I think it was around the time of the Baby M case, the case of a married couple who hired a surrogate mother. The surrogate was artificially inseminated, but refused to give up the child after the birth. The custody battle was all over the news back then. I don't know if that's why Suzanne's parents quit sending pictures, but the abrupt cutoff left me grief-stricken.

As I dig through a box in the closet, looking for letters and pictures, I find this poem that Brad wrote. He'd found me alone and crying on Suzanne's birthday in February 1995.

The breath of the winter
falls heavy on the boughs
beneath her window.

Her dream hand, gentle hand,
softly guides her sleepwalking
child back to bed.

She misses a time,
gone for good,
when simplicity ruled.

I put the poem back and see a plastic bag with a Santa Bear in it. It's the gift the social worker gave me to try to make me feel better. I had planned to give it to Suzanne when I saw her again someday. I ache all over. I wonder how she is. I dread the possibility that she's not okay, and that I was not there to protect her. Sometimes I feel so intensely about her that I think it will kill me. I don't regret giving her a better chance, but I will always regret not having seen her grow up.

As I dial Lutheran Social Services, I feel like my head is floating above my body. I have so many questions that have been nagging me for my entire adult life. *Were her new parents good to her? Was her life better with them than it would have been with me? Does she ever wonder about me? Does she wish to know me?*

Just as my Korean mother worried that I might not want to see her, I am terrified that Suzanne might not want to see me. Just as I worried that I might be a disappointment to my Korean family, I worry now that I will be a disappointment to my daughter.

Like my mother, I wish to hear my daughter's voice again. I want to tell her that I loved and valued her. I want to tell her how I wept the day I looked upon her beautiful face for the last time. I want to touch her and talk to her before I die.

I contact the adoption agency and leave all my information for my daughter if she should wish to contact me one day. For now, I must be patient and wait.

Nineteen

ANOTHER GOODBYE

TWO YEARS HAVE PASSED SINCE I REUNITED WITH MY biological family. The Korean Broadcasting System documentary aired several times in the fall of 2008, and became one of the KBS's most popular programs that year. This memoir has been translated into Korean and published, too. Millions of Koreans have seen the documentary or read the book.

In December 2009, Brad, the kids, and I flew back to Korea and spent Christmas with my family. Because many Koreans knew my story and my face, I'd been transformed into a minor celebrity. People pointed when I entered stores or walked down the street. One little girl in a store pulled her mother aside and whispered to her, and they both smiled as I passed. I liked the attention. It was difficult to return to my anonymous life in Minneapolis.

The autumn of 2010 is one of the mildest on record in Minnesota. The Midwestern rains come hard and early and then end abruptly. By the middle of October, Minneapolis is dry. The trees that line the streets, city lakes, and parks are awash in brilliant orange, yellow, and crimson, and the air is suffused with the smell of fallen leaves.

It's a slow Friday at work. The Minneapolis–St. Paul airport is nearly deserted. I am standing in the glass entryway, looking outside over the passenger drop-off area, when my cell phone rings. It's Sam. Although Sam has completed all the translation work in Korea, my family is still communicating with me through her.

"Are you able to talk now?" she asks. "I have some bad news for you."

I wonder what kind of news it could be. Four of my family members are planning to come to Minneapolis next summer, and I wonder whether they may have changed their minds. But Sam's voice sounds too grim to be reporting a cancelled vacation.

"I just talked with your brother, Chulsoo," Sam says. "He told me your father passed away about two hours ago. I'm sorry, Kelly, I know this must be hard."

I shouldn't be shocked. My Korean father has been cheating death for years.

"Are you OK?" she asks.

"Yeah, I'm OK." My reply is mechanical, because I'm not OK. I want to say more, but can't. Sam keeps talking, but her voice seems far away, as if she's speaking through a transistor radio somewhere down the hall. Visions of my father flash through my mind. The most vivid image is of him sleeping. That was when I checked his mouth for food in the middle of the night, placing my face close to his. I examine his cheekbones and his jaw, the thick bush of his black, Korean hair. I remember him lying on that mat, unable to get up, paralyzed by the senseless civil war. I recall his faded eyes when I visited him in the nursing home in Geumsan. He apologized for giving me up then. That was when he told me he loved me.

"Chulsoo said he understands that you might not be able to come, and that's OK. He doesn't want you to worry about it."

But I am worried about it. I want to go immediately. I know, however, that it will be almost impossible to make it to the other side of the planet in less than a couple of days.

"Yes, it would be difficult," I reply. "You know, Sam, we've been expecting this for a long time. That's why I took the second trip to visit him last December. I'm surprised he's hung on so long." Then we both pause, neither of us knowing what to say next. I think I ask something about how the family might be doing, but I'm not sure. Sam speaks some more—something comforting, no doubt—but I don't know what she says.

Outside, it's a beautiful day. Several of my coworkers are sitting on a bench, talking and laughing. Families are dropping off relatives, saying good-bye and hugging each other. The world is moving along without skipping a beat, as it always does when somebody dies, and as it should. It feels cruel, though, that my father is dead and no one here knows who he was, or that he was a hero and suffered greatly. No one here knows how much he loved me.

"I'll let you go now," Sam says. "I'm so sorry, Kelly. I feel for you."

Sam is one of the sweetest and kindest people I've ever met. I'm glad it was she who called.

"Thanks Sam. You have been so great."

"No problem. You guys are really special to me. I'm glad I can help."

I turn off my phone and lean against the window. I try to wrap my mind around the fact that I've lost my Korean father a second time—this time, forever. The little Korean girl remains alive in me, the daughter who still wants her father to come and rescue her. I'll have to let go of her, too.

I manage to make it to the employee bathroom before I fall apart. Two other TSA workers are in the bathroom, as I push my way into one of the stalls, sit down, and sob. It's an absurd scene—me sitting on a toilet in the Minneapolis–St. Paul International Airport employee bathroom with my uniform and badge on, crying like a baby.

My manager pops her head into the bathroom. "Miss Kelly, is that you?" she asks. Her voice is soft and filled with compassion. My partner for the day, Ray, has been kind enough to tell her what's going on and where I am.

"Yes," I croak, my voice rough from crying.

"Do you want to go home?"

"Yeah, I think I'd better," I reply.

"You get yourself together and see me when you're ready," she says.

The door closes and I cry some more, before collecting myself enough to make it to my car without falling apart. Within an hour, I'm standing in my living room with Brad's arms wrapped around me.

The next day is a whirlwind of tears and e-mail messages to and from my Korean family. Brad and I book seats on Asiana Airlines one minute, only to cancel them the next. Korean funerals can be drawn-out affairs, lasting days. My father's body will be prepared, cremated, and his ashes driven through parts of Korea for a variety of ceremonies. At least that's what I've been taught about Korean funerals. Since he was a war hero, my father's ashes will be buried at a special military cemetery, where he'll be given full military honors, complete with an honor guard. Because of all this, Chulsoo makes it clear that we'll arrive during the funeral. The family will be too busy to host us properly. They would be overwhelmed.

Between fits of sobbing and worrying about missing work, I'm in a daze. Brad drops me off at work on Sunday morning, but barely makes it a mile away from the airport before he has to turn around, pick me back up, and bring me home. I can't stop crying. I hadn't expected my Korean father's death to hit me so hard. Maybe it's because I owe so much of my identity and ego strength to him; maybe I missed out on so much of his life and I am feeling that loss.

Brad and the kids can see I'm struggling, so they pack a lunch and take me to the Walker Sculpture Garden. We lay out a blanket under a grove of small elms near Minneapolis's famous cherry-spoon sculpture and have a picnic. People mill around, enjoying the magnificent art and basking in the last beautiful weather before the arrival of the harsh Minnesota winter. The four of us eat cheese and French bread and talk about my Korean family, how we miss them and long to see them. We discuss my Korean father's death and remind ourselves how important family is.

Across the open space on the lawn, a young man and his girlfriend are making giant soap bubbles to entertain the children walking by. They're dressed as vagabonds: he with a top hat, old vest, and jeans; she with a gypsy skirt and bangles. It's not long before the two are surrounded by a mob of exuberant young faces. Max and Cici run over and join in the fun. I feel at peace for the first time since learning of my father's death.

We finish our picnic, pack up, and cross the Hennepin Avenue suspension bridge to Loring Park, a beautiful city green space with a small lake, rushes, and a large grassy area. We find a small pine tree, its lowest branches about three feet off the ground, with the cattails and the reeds that surround the lake providing a beautiful backdrop behind the tree. It's the perfect place to build an altar to honor my father.

Brad and the kids have shredded an old dress shirt into long, white strips. We each take turns tying strips to the lowest pine boughs. Then we place two pictures of my father carefully against the base of the tree. Brad fetches some wildflowers and some greens and reverently lays them in front of the pictures.

We each take a handful of rice to spread out in front of the flowers. Brad lights four sticks of incense, one for each of us, and we stick them into the ground to finish the shrine. Then we each write little notes to my father.

I'm surprised how much Max cries as he writes his note. I expected Cici to shed some tears, but Max is all boy. It's unusual to see him sob so intensely. In his little, eight-year-old handwriting, he writes, "Good-bye, Grandfather. I am going to miss you so much. Love Max." Cici writes that she'll miss him, too. Brad thanks him for giving him a loving wife.

I kneel down to lay my note at my father's altar. I bow under the pine branches as close to the ground as I can. My legs are bent beneath me, and my face is in my hands. I want to bless my father and wish him deep peace in the most profound way I can. "You are the love that kept me going," my note says. "Your love was like a beacon I could always count on. You gave me fire so I could survive during difficult times in my life. I love you, and I miss you. Myonghi."

Then we sit on a park bench a few yards away, facing the altar. We contemplate my Korean father's life and admire the shrine we built to honor him. Each time a group of park-goers walks by, they slow and turn silent out of deference to the four of us sitting on the bench, crying. The respect and compassion displayed by these strangers comforts me.

As the sun comes to rest on the western horizon, we leave the park, the incense still burning. Brad tells us that whatever happens to the altar now is meant to happen. I walk away with my husband and kids, and I don't look back. My father no longer belongs to this world. He certainly doesn't belong to me. Others will walk by and notice the rice and incense, the white strips of cloth hanging from the pine boughs and the pictures of the Asian man. They will wonder who he was.

Twenty

RECONNECTIONS

I LOVE MY HUSBAND DEARLY, AND I LOVE MY CHILDREN more than I thought I could possibly love anyone. But in the days after my father's death, I realize how truly wonderful the three of them are and how central to my life they've become. I've been robbed of attending my father's funeral, which has left me feeling separated and alienated from my Korean family again. Missing the ceremony made my father's death seem surreal and left me feeling helpless.

The ritual we performed in Loring Park, however, helped make the loss tangible, like it really happened and I was able to do something about it. I was hugged and told that I was loved a thousand times. I had been teetering on the verge of a chasm of deep sadness. My family had held me and pulled me back from falling in.

Within a few days I settle into a state of morose acceptance, accompanied by meltdowns here and there. It occurs to me that any anguish on my part is actually quite selfish. My father had been bedridden for years. Alzheimer's had ravaged his brain, and his muscles had atrophied until he'd become a curled-up mass of flesh. His suffering was over. I could just as easily be happy for him. He was truly better off.

Four days after my father's death, I'm feeling better. I come home from work and hug my kids. I change out of my uniform, pour a glass of wine, and head for the living room. Brad is in the office with the door closed. I can see him through the panes of the French door talking on the phone to someone about something that appears to be important. He's hunched over the desk with an intense look on his face.

I don't go in and kiss him like I usually do when I get home from work. I sit down and begin surfing the television channels for a suitable program to help me unwind from a busy day working for Homeland Security. Within a few minutes, Brad hangs up the phone and steps out of the office.

"How was your day at work?" he asks in a tone of voice that implies he has reason to ask beyond general cordiality. His face is animated, as if he has something to tell.

"It was OK," I say, my voice trailing off.

"How are you feeling?"

"I'm fine. What is it?"

Then he blurts out something that I've been waiting to hear for over twenty-four years. "I found your daughter. I found Suzanne. I was just talking to her adopted mother on the phone."

I don't know what to say. Of course, I've always wanted to see my lost daughter, but it's been less than a week since my Korean father's death. I'm already so emotionally drained.

"God, Brad. I don't know if I can handle this."

"I know. I'm sorry. The timing isn't the best."

"How did you find her?"

Brad launches into an explanation of how he used her first name, birth date, and the county in which she was born. He triangulated these three things and searched a hundred different web sites. At first, he found some young woman in the Philippines with a matching name and birth date. He found a picture of her and decided that she looked exactly like me, except for her nose. He sent an e-mail to her, but she replied that she'd never been to the United States.

Then Brad tells me how he contacted a genealogist friend. She searched a genealogy database and found a birth certificate matching the three bits of information. She told Brad that it wasn't unusual for birth records to be amended retroactively to include the adopted parents' names. Brad took the two parents' names and searched the Internet. He wasn't able to find anything about the woman whose name was listed on the birth certificate, but he eventually discovered a high-school graduation-reunion site with the man's updated contact information.

"There was a phone number included with the information," Brad continues. "So I dialed it. I didn't actually think I was calling Suzanne's parents. I figured it was a long shot and that someone on the other end might know something. I introduced myself and said that I was looking for a girl named Suzanne who was adopted in '86 and whose biological mother was Korean."

"What did she say?" I ask, feeling a little disappointed that it hadn't been me who'd made the first contact.

"She got really angry. She said, 'Who is this? You're invading our privacy.' And I thought, *bingo!* I hit the jackpot. I told her that I'd hang up and never call back if she wanted. I told her she could have full control. Then she started asking questions about your health, whether you used to smoke or not, things like that. She asked about your family health history, and it felt good that I was able to tell her about your biological mother and father."

I picture a woman with silver, wavy hair and an angry expression. I find myself worrying that Brad has bungled the first contact and alienated Suzanne's mother. I fight the urge to scold him. But he's worked so hard to find Suzanne, I don't want to be ungrateful.

"Then what did she say?" I ask.

"She kind of switched back and forth between asking questions and telling me that I was invading their privacy. I can't say that I blame her. Some knucklehead calls out of the blue and says that he's married to your daughter's biological mother. I'd be defensive, too."

"She's being protective."

"That's right," Brad says. "In the end, she said that I sounded like a nice guy and that she would give Suzanne my phone number and blog address. Anyway, we've got Suzanne's last name now."

Brad lifts his eyebrows suggestively. At first, I don't understand what he's getting at. Then I realize that Suzanne's last name is the key to finding information about her on the Internet. I jump up, and we both make a dash for the computer.

Within minutes Brad and I are searching the World Wide Web with my daughter's newly discovered full name. The first search turns up an old web site that lists a young woman as a tutor for children. A thumbnail picture shows a beautiful girl with dark hair, wearing a crown of some sort. The picture is distorted because of the angle at which it's been taken. I study the eyes and smile. I want this young woman to be my daughter, but I don't recognize the features. It says she is twenty-two years of age, which means that the site is about two years old. It notes that she has been teaching preschool kids for five years. I don't think it is her.

We search again and find another web site address that includes her name. With the press of a button, a beautiful young face appears on the computer screen. She has faultless skin and dark, almond-shaped eyes. Her smile is perfect. Her hand has been placed on her head for the photo, and she's looking over her shoulder with her bangs flipped back over her wrist. I recognize her immediately from the pictures her parents sent me after the adoption. I'm certain that she is my daughter.

The web site says that she is a coloratura soprano, that she graduated from a local college with a degree in theater, has appeared in several local theater productions, and loves to sing at weddings. There are pictures of her singing and acting in productions such as *The Fantasticks, The Titanic, The King and I,* and *Top Girls*. Most magical of all is a video stream of her singing. I move the cursor to her picture and push the play button. Suddenly, I'm watching my precious baby singing a Stephen Sondheim song, "Green Finch and Linnet Bird," from *Sweeney Todd*.

> *Green finch and linnet bird,*
> *Nightingale, blackbird,*
> *How is it you sing?*
> *How can you jubilate,*
> *Sitting in cages,*
> *Never taking wing?*
> *Outside the sky waits,*
> *Beckoning, beckoning,*
> *Just beyond the bars.*
> *How can you remain,*
> *Staring at the rain,*
> *Maddened by the stars?*

One second her voice is as soft as air against rose petals, the next it rises like a choir. Her sweet personality is revealed with every expression, and every turn of her head shows me that she's gentle and kind. The little angel of my memories has grown into the real thing. She's perfect.

I can hardly breathe. I weep tears of unspeakable joy. I can't help but think my father is orchestrating this, that he's taking care of his little girl. Only a parent who has given up a child can know how it feels, and he understands. He was released from that crumbling old body, and is now making this happen as a gift for me.

But hearing Suzanne's voice on a computer or seeing her on video isn't enough. I want to touch her, to hold her again and explain why I gave her up. I want her to understand. I'm tempted to use the information on the web site to contact her, but Brad has promised her mother that she'll have control. I will have to wait.

I'll always have a scar on my heart. I missed my daughter's childhood and will never be able to get the time back. I accept that dull, chronic pain as a consequence of the choice I made over two decades ago. But after discovering that she's well and appears to be thriving, I can forgive myself . . . at least a little bit.

Of course, the first correspondence between us doesn't occur as quickly as I would like. Two weeks pass without a word—no phone call, no e-mail, nothing. I wake up in the mornings feeling wonderful that I've found her, only to go to bed each night sobbing, because she hasn't called. I start becoming paranoid. I wonder if Suzanne's mother hasn't passed along the information. Maybe she thinks Suzanne isn't ready or that contact with me will only complicate their lives. Maybe Brad was too aggressive and has frightened them away.

One morning, I wake up and decide that I just can't stand waiting anymore. I send a note via the contact page on her web site. I find her on Facebook, too, and craft a cryptic message that won't embarrass her if someone else reads it. I make sure to leave my e-mail address so she can drop a note, instead of having to make an awkward phone call. I still don't know when or if she'll contact me, and the anticipation continues to drive me crazy.

The next couple of days are hell. I check my e-mail again and again for any word. I resist checking at work because I fell apart there after learning of my father's death, and I don't want TSA management to think I'm unstable. Nonetheless, I make frequent trips to the employee bathrooms to cry, or simply to calm down. Sometimes, when I get off work, I cry all the way home. At night, while lying in bed, I cry some more. I'm an emotional wreck. The tears are always just below the surface, and there's a constant cramp in my throat.

I decide it would be better to start talking to others besides Brad. I'm so needy, and he's already done more than his share of listening. Before I found Suzanne, talking about her always made me feel worse. It always made the pain of losing her more intense. But now, talking about her helps relieve the anxiety—or, at least it does when I talk to Brad. I decide that I will have to put my guilt and shame aside. I write a letter to my good friend Kyo in Japan. Then I tell my Vietnamese friend TuQuynh, my Korean friend Carrie, and my Tibetan friend Tenzing. Eventually, I let my friends Esther, Isabelle, and Annie know. It helps to break the secret.

One day at work I feel the phone ringing in my pocket. I'm in the middle of questioning a traveler, a young businessman, whom I've stopped for a random screening. I let the answering system take the call. When the phone rings a second time, I know it's Brad and that it has something to do with Suzanne. I ask the young man for his identification and his ticket; I search his bag and ask him several mundane questions, all the while monitoring his anxiety level, mannerisms, and facial expressions. Going insane about my newly found daughter is no excuse for shirking my responsibility; my work is about protecting people. I make sure all of the man's identification checks out, and send him on his way.

I excuse myself and sit by some public phones near an empty storefront in a busy section of the main terminal. I look in both directions, in front of me and behind me through the crowd, to make sure that none of my coworkers can see me should I cry. Then I call Brad. As the phone rings, I work the possibilities through my mind: *Did she write back? Is she angry? Does she want to see me?* I struggle to keep my expectations low.

"Hello," Brad says. "Guess what? I have some good news."

I pretend not to assume, that he might be calling for some other reason: one of the kids did well on a school assignment or something good happened to him at work. "What is it?" I ask.

"Suzanne replied. She wrote a very sweet e-mail. She's interested in meeting you."

There is a God, I think, *and he loves me dearly*. I lean against the wall and take a deep breath. A warm sensation pulsates through my body as the tears roll down my smiling face. I'm tempted to have Brad read the e-mail over the phone, but I won't be able to control my emotions. My thoughts run wild with future possibilities: Suzanne coming through the front door of my house, excited about something she bought and wanting to show it to me. I picture us standing in a kitchen together. I imagine me showing her how to make soup and her giggling and talking to me with Cici and Max joining in. I dream of taking her to Korea and introducing her to my Korean mother, all of us sitting on my mother's living room floor—eating kimchi, laughing, talking, and going over all we missed in each other's lives. I see the two of us together in France, sitting at some sidewalk café, drinking crème café and eating salad *niçoise*. We visit the museums together, walking the Champs-Élysées and the Champ de Mars.

When I arrive home, I go directly to the computer and read her e-mail.

Sent: Tue, October 26, 2010 5:26:10 PM
Subject: Re: birth mother
Hello Kelly,

It is absolutely surreal to hear from you and see your picture on my Facebook. Yes, my mother did tell me about you and was going to tell your husband my e-mail address! I would like to meet you as well, though I think it would be best to take it slow and perhaps get to know each other a little through e-mail and on the phone at first. Hopefully this is OK with you! I think it may be too overwhelming for me to immediately jump into meeting with you, but please know that I am so happy to hear from you and am very interested in finally seeing you and getting to talk to you! :-)

Thank you for finding me! Also, I have seen your husband's blog and want to tell you that you and your children are extremely beautiful!

I'm looking forward to hearing more from you.

Suzie

"Don't worry," I say to Brad, as the tears stream down my cheeks. "These are tears of joy I'm crying, not sad ones."

I jump up and run to get a tissue. I stand, looking in the mirror above the bathroom vanity, thinking back to the old stroller I wheeled Suzanne around in. It was the spring and summer of 1986. It wore out because I walked her for miles nearly every day—until my feet were sore and the stroller's plastic wheels had worn away. I thought that fresh air was the best thing for her. There was no one to teach me how important it was to hold a baby. I always regretted not holding her more.

I clean myself up and return to the computer and Brad.

"I can't believe how much her e-mail is like the first one you sent to your Korean mother," he says. "Gawd, it's practically a cut and paste."

The similarities are truly amazing. I was happy to hear from my Korean mother, too; but I'd wanted to go slow because I wasn't sure how I felt.

I sit down and write my reply.

Sent: Tue, Oct 26, 2010 9:54 pm
Subject: Re: birth mother
Dear Suzie,

I can't believe that I've finally found you. I am so happy to hear from you. Of course, I understand you wanting to take it slow. Whatever you want is OK with me, but I am quite anxious to see you.

I want you to know that I have never stopped thinking about or loving you. (My emotions are very big right now, and I don't want to overwhelm you.) I've been to your web site and saw you singing. You are amazing. I've been a wreck since we found you. I've been doing a lot of crying. I realize that your feelings might not be as big as mine, so I want to make sure that I respect that. I realize that you don't remember me. If you are interested, I was interviewed on a radio show about my life, *Dick Gordon and the Story*. In that interview, I mention you. I'll put the link below. It will inform you a little bit about me. I will talk to you as much as you are willing, and I will meet with you whenever you decide that you are ready.

I am so happy! (And nervous.)

Love,
Kelly

I click the send button, sit back, and take a deep breath. The second broken part of my life is coming full circle. I reunited with my Korean family after thirty-seven-years and now my daughter after twenty-four. I spend the next day in a frenetic state of cautious elation, thrilled that my foot is in the door but unsure about when or if she will invite me through it.

Sent: Wed, October 27, 2010

Dear Kelly,

I am so surprised you have seen my video! :-) I have a lot of them. It's kind of something I do as a hobby that relieves stress and makes me happy.

I am very glad you like it.

To be quite honest, I never thought you would try to find me, so when my mother told me that your husband called I was really shocked and didn't know what to feel. Ultimately I am very nervous, excited, and really happy that you have found me. I would love to meet you within the next month or so if that is alright with you!

Your radio interview was extremely interesting, and it was fun to be able to hear your voice. What an amazingly unique and incredible life you have!

My parents told me very early on that I was adopted and am half Korean, and that you were first generation from Korea which makes me second generation. I had no idea you were 5 years old when you came to America, for some reason I always thought you would have been much younger. To actually have a recollection of your previous life and family is something I cannot even begin to imagine.

My parents listened to the interview as well. They said that the way you laugh at the end of a sentence is similar to the way I laugh at the end of a sentence, and that your story about biting was similar to when I was younger and I bit a couple of people as well.

I am really looking forward to seeing you and being able to notice that we have similar smiles, or that I have your eyes, or something of that nature since I have never really experienced genetic similarities before!

What are you nervous about?

I am mostly nervous that I will be disappointing for you to meet. Maybe you have some expectations of what I will be like or what I will look like that won't be met. I just hope you won't be let down.

Anyway, it is such an indescribable feeling to write to you, and to hear back from you. You have often been the topic of my thoughts and conversations with dear friends. Never in a negative way, always spoken of with curiosity and wonder.

These next two weeks or so I will be kind of busy. I have just bought my very own condo, and will be moving in, painting, cleaning, and the works, so if I don't respond right away it could be because my Internet isn't connected at my new place!

Talk to you soon!

Suzie

Sent: Thu, Oct 28, 2010

Dear Suzie,

You could never be a disappointment to me. I am already very pleased with everything about you. I can't believe what a wonderful young woman you have grown to be. I'm extremely proud of you. Your parents did such a great job. I'm so grateful that they took such good care of you. Please know that I never wanted to give you up. It's too early to dump too much on you now. There will be time to explain later. There are things that are too hard to say in a letter, let alone in an e-mail. Just know that the day I gave you up was the most painful day of my life. I've always felt horrible about it, and I've always prayed that someday I'd see you again. If the question about whether you were loved ever has entered your mind, yes you were. You were loved dearly. Words don't express how much.

I'm not sure that I can articulate why I'm nervous. I feel guilty. I feel ashamed. Most of all, I'm afraid you will be disappointed with who I am or that you will be angry with me. (By the way, if you are angry, it's OK. I understand.)

I am so happy to hear that you want to meet with me within the next month. I can't believe that we are communicating. I have to pinch myself to believe it's finally true. You and I are going to meet soon!

You do have my eyes. I could see it on the videos. The first time I saw you, my first thought was that you were so beautiful. Your web page is quite nice, too.

I'm glad you had a chance to listen to my interview and learn a little about me. I feel like I know a little about you from watching your video and seeing your web site. You have such a beautiful voice. My Korean mom said that she thought I would be a singer some day. Unfortunately, my beautiful voice went away with puberty. Obviously, yours has not.

I met my biological family for the first time in 2008. I had such a wild range of emotions then. I didn't remember my mother, and that was hard for me. I did remember my sisters and my father, though. And I remember chasing my little brother around, trying to pick him up. My Korean father passed away just weeks ago. I am so glad I was able to see him before he died. He was your biological grandfather. He was a hero in the Korean Civil War and a wonderful man.

Someday I would love to see you perform. If it doesn't make you nervous. Also, congratulations on your new condo. I'm sure it's very nice.

This may sound strange or inappropriate, but I feel like I should be helping you paint and clean! :) Both Cici and Max have known about you since the beginning. Brad and I have always told them that they have a half sister out there somewhere. They've seen your pictures and seen me crying. (I have a few pictures of you as a child, your first dress, and your hospital bracelet.) They are very excited to meet you someday. Brad is very excited, too.

It's hard for me to end this communication. I want to tell you so much, and I can hardly wait to see you.

With Love,

Kelly

After several months of e-mails, texts, and Facebook messages, we finally decide to meet on Thursday, December 23, 2010. It's a beautifully sunny winter morning. We settle on a restaurant called The Cheesecake Factory in the Minneapolis suburb of Edina. It's connected to one of the Twin Cities' nicest shopping malls and located within a short driving distance from both of our homes. It has good food, a beautiful décor, and secluded booths in which a mother can talk to her daughter without worrying about other people listening or watching.

Seventeen inches of snow have fallen just a few days ago, and everything is covered with a brilliant, sparkling white blanket. The temperature is in the twenties—balmy compared to the typical Minnesota mid-December winter. The plows have piled the snow high to the sides of the roads, making them constricted and hard to navigate. I have to keep my mind on driving, which proves a welcome distraction from how nervous I am.

As I pull into the mall parking lot, I suddenly have a strange feeling—a premonition—that I'll see Suzanne before we both enter the restaurant. Just then, a pickup truck pulls in next to me. I look over to see if it might be her, but a man jumps out. Another car pulls in, but there is an elderly woman inside.

I grab the bag of gifts I've brought along, get out of my car, and head toward the restaurant. About ten feet ahead of me, I can see a young woman in a full-length, bright-pink coat, who seems to be going in the same direction. She has long, dark brown hair, with bangs pushed to the sides. It's her. She's even more beautiful in real life than in her pictures. She recognizes me and smiles.

"Oh, my gosh. It's you," I say, trying to sound as offhand as possible.

She smiles welcomingly. "I was wondering if that was you, too."

"Can I give you a hug?" I ask.

"Sure." She opens her arms and lets me in.

I've finally arrived. I feel like I'm in heaven. I want to stay close to my daughter, forever. I close my eyes and picture her little feet and hands and those beautiful brown eyes looking up at me twenty-four years ago. I want to cry, but don't. Instead, I tear myself away without letting her know that I don't want to let go. I settle for that first fleeting hug with a wish and a prayer that there'll be many more to come.

I step back to have a look at her. We stand studying each other for a few seconds. She looks much more like me in real life than in the pictures. She greatly resembles Cici. I should probably say something, but can't think of anything appropriate.

"How was your drive in?" I ask.

"It wasn't too bad," she responds.

I notice she has a photo album in her hand. "I'm so glad you brought pictures," I say.

She pulls them out and starts showing them to me, right there on the sidewalk.

"Here's a picture of me performing," she says. It's a picture of her with face paint on, wearing a white harlequin shirt. "I was a narrator in a show. I was really nervous because it was one of my first plays. I wasn't doing something with the group, and I had to narrate on my own."

It's hard for me to pay attention to what she's saying. I just want to stand here and study her beautiful face. I want to drink in her facial expressions, and savor the wonderful way she forms her words.

She shows me a picture of her sitting at a fireplace hearth with her mother. Christmas stockings are fastened to the bricks behind them, and they're both holding cats. Her mother is pretty, with a beautiful complexion and a warm smile. She's far younger than I had imagined. Suzie's father is seated at their feet, holding a dog. He has a strong, trustworthy face. It's not surprising that Suzie turned out to be such a sweet girl. *Thank God for her parents*, I think. I owe so much to them.

All at once, I notice her hand is shaking.

"Oh, it's so cold," I say. "Do you want to stand out here and wait for the restaurant to open, or would you like to go and wait in the mall?"

She looks relieved. "Oh yes, if you don't mind, I'd rather go inside."

I walk with her to the entrance of the mall, still not knowing quite how to behave. Should I say clever things or just let it be? I have to suppress the urge to grab her, squeeze her, and cry— to repress the urge to scream with joy. She, on the other hand, seems to be relatively comfortable and relaxed.

We enter the mall, and I start asking her questions. I don't know what I'm saying, exactly; it is as if I'm high on some kind of drug. My mind is being pulled in so many different directions, as if I have a Rolodex in my head that's spinning out of control. I keep thinking of her as a little baby and wondering if anything I did all those years ago might have hurt her. I wonder if anything I didn't do might have hurt her. I keep thinking about how sweet she is and how relieved I am that a nice couple adopted her. I feel lucky that she isn't angry at me.

I see the hostess through the restaurant window unlocking the restaurant door, and in a moment, we're seated at a booth, and I'm able to take a closer look at her. Her hair is fine and shiny, and her skin is cream colored, a bit darker than it appeared in her web photo. A hint of soft freckles covers her nose and parts of her cheeks just like mine, but she has a Caucasian nasal bridge, unlike me. Her eyes are just like Cici's. When she flashes her sweet smile it reveals perfectly straight, sparkling white teeth. Her hands are delicate and gently shaped. She speaks in a high, sweet tone. A blue, bejeweled pendant about the size of a matchbox hangs from a chain around her neck. It has a picture in it.

"Whose picture is that?" I ask.

"It's Snow White," she replies. "She is my favorite Disney character."

Then I remember that in October one of her e-mails said that her Halloween costume had been Snow White. Some of the songs on her website are Disney songs as well.

"I loved Disney when I was young, too," I say. "Even as an adult, I loved *The Little Mermaid*."

I pull out the bag of gifts.

"Oh, I didn't bring anything for you," she says.

"Just being here with you is my gift," I respond.

One of the gifts is a bracelet wrapped in a gorgeous, soft pink box with a silver, embossed oval pattern. I bought the box in Korea.

"I hope you like this," I say, handing it to her. "It's kind of girly-girl. But I'm kind of a girly-girl."

She laughs. "Yes, really. I like it. I like girly things, too."

"Cici and I have ones just like it," I add, knowing full well that the bracelets are icons for the bond between the three of us. Just then, the tears begin to well up in my eyes again, and I fight them back. There's no way I'm going to frighten her away. I can sense that she doesn't want this first meeting to be too heavy. I pretend that I'm not dying inside.

I give her an ornate business-card holder from Korea, one that I bought at the Incheon Airport gift shop. I also give her a keychain with pink rhinestones and a little, high-heeled shoe and heart on it, which she seems to really love. Finally, I give her pictures of Cici and Max, her half siblings.

"They're so cute," she says, holding the pictures in her hand.

"Now that I'm seeing you face to face, you and Cici look so much alike."

"Yah, I think we look alike, too."

"There's no doubt that you're related."

I've always loved this child, and now I'm relieved that I like her, too. She's such a lady. Before I know it, an hour has passed. The restaurant is filled, and the waitress has returned several times, asking if we need anything else and hinting that we're lingering too long.

"Hey, it looks like we should go," I say. "Would you like to walk around the mall and shop with me?"

"I'd love to do that," Suzanne says.

There are no angels or trumpets heralding from the heavens right now, but there should be. Suzie actually wants to spend more time with me. She doesn't want to escape. Maybe she's just being kind. Maybe she can read me better than I think and she's having pity on the woman with the broken heart. Regardless, this day is the culmination of twenty-four years of hopes and wishes, and I'm going to make the most of it. I'm going to spend as much time with my daughter as she will allow.

We browse the shirts at H&M. We look at boots and blouses in Macy's, and we peruse kitchen gadgets in Marshall's. I offer to buy her a pair of slippers and a sweater, but she won't allow it. Eventually, she lets me buy her a bag of organic vitamin C lollipops. We walk through the shopping center casually, something mothers and daughters do every day throughout the world. It's been over three hours.

"I'm sorry, Suzie," I say, "but I have to go. I left Cici at Brad's work, and Max is at a friend's birthday party. I'm so glad we got to spend some time together."

"I had a really good time with you," she says. "I really enjoyed myself."

We embrace, and I hold on as long as I can. I finally allow myself to release just a few tears.

"Even though I wasn't there to see you grow up," I say, "I've always loved you."

She smiles. "I'm so glad that I finally got to meet you."

As I drive home, I'm so happy, yet I'm still in such pain. I have no memory of her first steps or first words. I never got to dress her in her favorite dress or walk her to the park. I wasn't there to put her on the bus for her first day of school, or kiss her goodnight and tuck her in. She will always be my daughter, but I will never be her mother.

I remember all of the judgment and condemnation that was directed toward me, the runaway who got pregnant and had a baby when she was a teen. I've always felt shameful about my past, but I've never been ashamed that I conceived and gave birth to that beautiful child. I've never regretted that wonderful gift, not for a second. The yoke of shame I bear is that I failed to live up to the title of "mother." I failed to give my daughter a home and to keep her safe. I did not keep her warm and fed. I did not hold her.

This day, my forever regret has receded a little. My shame has eased. When I felt Suzie's arms around me, a sliver of hope worked its way into my flesh, and will burrow further if I can let go of the past just a little bit. Maybe she and I can claim something fruitful in the future. Maybe she and I can have something together.

Twenty-One

MOVING ON

I**T IS A SUNDAY EVENING, MONTHS AFTER MEETING SUZIE.** She and her boyfriend Ryan are over for dinner. I'd wanted to express my love by cooking for them, but I'd had to work this morning. We settle for Chinese takeout. No one seems to mind. Being with Suzie is so much more casual now, so much more relaxed.

After dinner, Cici leads her big sister into her bedroom to show off her stuffed animals, her Justin Bieber poster, and her jewelry. Max is practically jumping out of his skin waiting for Ryan to play video games with him. He's been anticipating the visit for days. .

Suzie eventually makes her way to my living room couch. Ryan cuddles up warmly by her side. They're holding hands, smiling, and talking about their lives together. I'm in a chair, perpendicular to the couch. Brad is sitting in the chair next to me. Every time Suzie smiles, I see a part of me in her. Every time I look at her, I feel a warm surge of joy fill my heart. We spend the evening together. They leave, and I can hardly wait until the next time.

Suzie's mother Pam—the angel who nurtured my precious flower and now a friend of mine—gave me an album with some of the baby pictures I'd sent along with the adoption papers back in 1986. It turns out that she hadn't stopped sending me letters and pictures of Suzie. The Baby M case had had nothing to do with it. My forwarded address had never made it to the adoption agency. Pam had always been open to communication, and she had wondered and worried about what had happened to me. She and her husband had sent pictures and letters for over eight years.

The album includes a picture of me holding Suzie at three weeks, and two pictures of Suzie's biological father sitting in a chair, holding little Suzie, with me standing behind. There are eleven other pictures of Suzie alone. In several, she is smiling, which is a relief. I don't remember her smiling much. Maybe that was a fabrication created by my grief.

One of the pictures is of little Suzie standing, holding onto a table. She was doing that before I gave her up. I remember now. She was pretty shaky, and I had to help her. But she was so proud that she could stand up.

I turn the pages and see several pictures of the foster mother holding Suzie, and finally, a photograph of Pam holding Suzie their first day together. It's dated December 15, 1986. I met my new parents just four days short of fifteen years earlier, on December 19, 1971. The parallels are striking. Pam appears to be every bit as excited as my American mother was. *Thank God for Pam*, I think. I'm so grateful that my baby was taken in by a loving mother.

I've been struggling lately to make sense of all that I've been through. Perhaps the meaning has something to do with the power of love, a force far deeper and more profound than genetics or biology. I remember my American mother caressing my hands once, speculating whose side of the family contributed the shape of my fingers. She'd forgotten that she had adopted me. It didn't matter that I was born from a different woman on the opposite side of the planet. She loved me. Pam loves Suzie. The world turns.

Regardless of the meaning I'm supposed to take away, I pray for the parentless children—frightened and confused—who cry in the night because they don't know what will become of them. I pray for them, and think back to that Korean orphanage four decades ago. I remember hearing their suppressed crying. I hope that my story, if they hear of it, will be of some comfort to them now, especially for those whose stories didn't end as happily as mine. And I wish that every broken-hearted mother who has ever given a child away could eventually heal as I have healed, like my Korean mother has healed. I wish that every father who has lost a child can say "I love you" before he dies, like my father did.

A matter of months ago I could only dream about my eldest daughter. Now I can see her, hear her, touch her. I don't have to worry about whether she was loved. I don't wonder if she's lonely or afraid. I no longer dread that I made a horrible mistake by giving her over to another family to love. I did the right thing.

Once every month or so, my Korean family e-mails, telling me how much they love and miss me. They drop hints about wanting me to come back to South Korea, and they send pictures of my Korean nephews and nieces. The little ones are growing so fast. I e-mail back, saying I love them, too, and that I plan to visit as soon as possible. I will tell them about Suzie soon. So much has come together. So much has healed.

Now, when someone speculates about my history and how fortunate I've been, I have to admit that I am indeed lucky.